WHAT TO EAT AFTER THE APOCALYPSE

VLADIMIR STEFAN

First published by Vladimir Stefan, 2025

Copyright © 2025 by Vladimir Stefan

All rights reserved. No part of this publication may be reproduced, stored or transmitted in any form or by any means, electronic, mechanical, photocopying, recording, scanning, or otherwise without written permission from the publisher. It is illegal to copy this book, post it to a website, or distribute it by any other means without permission.

This novel is entirely a work of fiction. The names, characters and incidents portrayed in it are the work of the author's imagination. Any resemblance to actual persons, living or dead, events or localities is entirely coincidental.

Designations used by companies to distinguish their products are often claimed as trademarks. All brand names and product names used in this book and on its cover are trade names, service marks, trademarks and registered trademarks of their respective owners. The publishers and the book are not associated with any product or vendor mentioned in this book. None of the companies referenced within the book have endorsed the book.

First edition

Paperback ISBN: 978-1-0686126-2-6;

E-book ISBN: 978-1-0686126-3-3;

Cover art by Christian Storm

Back cover art by Leyla Hunn

INTRODUCTION

Over a year ago, I released my debut novel into the world. I introduced you to Dom, his band of misfits, and perhaps most importantly, to Mango. I imagined a world not too distant from our own.

In the time since I wrote that, far too much of what I thought was speculative has become disturbingly real. What once felt like dystopian exaggeration now feels increasingly familiar. Within a year, many parts of the Western world have accelerated toward authoritarianism with breathtaking speed. We witness genocide livestreamed, enabled by allies. We see children starve and people dehumanised, and still we're told it's justified. Inequality is no longer hidden, but institutionalised. We're the forest, but we keep voting for the axe, for its handle is made of wood.

So I find myself asking:

How do you write dystopia when dystopia feels

like the present?

If I seem to be writing prophecies, then let me try this one:

We will one day escape this nightmare. We will move toward a future where the many don't just survive, but thrive.

And until it exists in reality, and no matter how long it takes, I'll keep writing it into fiction. Sharp-edged, politically charged, and defiantly hopeful.

In *What to Eat After the Apocalypse*, we return to Dom and the gang, where the adrenaline of revolution has passed, and harder questions begin. What comes after? How do we build in stillness, not movement? And is it possible to protect peace without repeating the mistakes of the past?

Welcome to the Commune of Hounslow.

Dedicated to those holding onto community in times of division.

APPETIZER

"Keep pushing!" I shout with every ounce of energy left.

This was what we fought so hard for. From atop Big Ben, the city dazzles, and the thousands of people marching in tandem below create an atmospheric scene as the sun slowly descends in the faraway west. You can smell the gunpowder and hear hundreds of chats, cheers, and chants.

"Free-dom, Free-dom" echoes through the crowd.

From being in the dark, fearing for our future, hiding in the underground and planning rogue attacks on whatever government forces remained, we are now out, loud and pushing back against the oppressors as an unstoppable collective. Tension had built over the past weeks, but the *"have-nots"* finally united and had each other's backs. A tear runs down my cheek as I see the number of people flocking through the streets leading to the Houses of Parliament. None of our enemies in sight; it's a clear path to an all-boarded-up house of former fascist representatives. Now they feel how we felt all these weeks. We march on.

The cheers are getting louder as more people advance and push inside Westminster's outer courts. I look towards the horizon, and the sky slowly clears up as the clouds of smoke start dispersing. My hand is shaking as I radio Patience,

"Are you guys streaming this?" The corners of my mouth tremble, and I cannot stop smiling.

"Yes, mate," she says as I hear people celebrating around her, "We love the views from the drones!"

"Okay—I'm going to head down there and…"

A siren is heard from far away, slowly fading in towards us. A few more sirens sound closer to Westminster. As more people hear the alarms, the loud cheers of revolution start to fade out, and everyone starts checking their surroundings slowly. I can hear my radio trying to connect, buzzing until clear.

"Dom—what's going on?" asks an unsuspecting Patience. I don't answer as I check the surroundings from up high. After a few seconds of deafening silence from the crowd, people start chanting again. I rejoice with a cheer, but as I turn north, I spot a couple of missiles rising from the ground. Their vapour trails ascend and start curving, approaching us. Below, people cheer, unaware of it all.

"Shit, Chris—the clock, now! Ring the bell."

"What?" he asks, while I point toward the missiles. "Shit—on it."

Chris slides toward the chamber of the bell and pulls the rope. The clock starts making its characteristic gongs. "Faster, Chris!"

The noise now feels more urgent. People are turning towards Big Ben, so I try my best to shout: "Retreat, back to the underground!"

Some heed my warning, while others are too far ahead of the crowd to return and keep pushing inside Parliament.

I take a deep breath, hoping to help my voice get louder,

"Retreat, there's …"

BOOM. A few hundred yards away. The situation kicks in, and panic starts to take place. Chris rings a few more bells and urges me to follow him down.

I shout one more "Retreat!" before descending and making my way towards the underground.

BOOM. BOOM. Two more rounds hit the same area.

People are swarming at the tube entrance, the stronger moving further, faster. There's a great deal of pushing and shoving. Behind me, I feel the force of hundreds trying to push forward and get to safety. Among the shouts and screams, a few voices urge the masses to calm down, but the situation is anything but. Pressed from all sides, I try to free my hands enough to reach into my pockets. I grab my radio and set it on all frequencies,

"London—stay underground. Missiles have been launched."

Close to Westminster's gates, I see Mrs Patel, the former shopkeeper, now a frontline resistance member, frozen in the crowd, standing still as hundreds panic around her. I make my way towards her, nudging people away. The death of Mr Patel a few days ago struck her hard, and her desire to help always overcompensates her need for grief—that old-school immigrant mentality of working hard despite all adversity. With one hand, I grab her shoulder and get her moving. She clings to my arm as we move with the masses. As more missiles strike, the buildings around us start collapsing. The air feels heavy, and I'm sweating, but we finally manage to get to safety with dust in our lungs and clothes.

.....

It's been a few hours, and the barrage of missiles seems to have stopped. Only the murmur of people looking for friends or trying to reach other underground stations remains. A few more people have been coming in throughout, coughing and wearing dusty clothes. From what they are saying, these are the same green gas explosives that started this whole ordeal. It is difficult to calm people as many miss friends or relatives, and everyone seems hugely discouraged. After all, was this assault on Westminster worth it, or did we expose ourselves as a massive target, giving them the perfect opportunity to strike as many of us at once?

I've been trying to reach Hounslow West but with little success. All the frequencies seem busy and hard to connect to. People from all walks of life are with me. A bunch of lads in their early twenties, all rocking football t-shirts, sit at the platform's edge, drinking a few cans of beer, loitering and chanting in complete contrast to the sentiment of the many taking refuge from the bombs. I walk towards them, hoping to take my mind off the situation for a second.

"Alright, lads, mind if I have one?" I say, pointing towards the beers.

One of the guys is checking me from head to toe and doing a visual count of the number of cans divided by the number of drinkers. Ultimately, we don't know how long we'll be here, so one has to divide equally. The others turn their heads towards him like a mob of meerkats, awaiting his decision. The leader, I suppose.

"Are you Dom?" he asks, and I nod, confirming. He smiles. "Of course, my guy, here, have a couple! Is Gerrard around too?"

I shake my head and accept the beers. "Only Chris and Mrs Patel, the rest are back in Hounslow. Thank you, lads."

"Oi, Dom," he says, "We'll get through this too, mate."

The mob of meerkats nods in unison, supporting the sentiment. I don't know why, but I needed this lad's confidence. He might be a few beers deep and a Manchester United fan, but he's right. If he can watch that team get battered every week, yet still follow them, then perhaps optimism is just a gravy of belief and loyalty. I make my way towards Chris, who is sitting on the tracks. I turn my head slightly, back to the lads,

"Boys—everyone is pretty down—could you, I don't know, do some chanting to get everyone's spirits up?"

The self-appointed leader smiles back at me. He gets it. He turns towards his gang as an orchestra conductor, and as I make my way towards Chris, I hear a growing tune.

"Oh, when the lads go marching in; Oh, when the lads go marching in; I want to be in Westminster; When the lads go marching in."

As I sit down next to Chris and Mrs Patel, more and more people join in. The platform is lively now, and while there is a lot of suffering and disbelief, the song brings us together a bit. The tune slowly transitions to the classic Italian anti-fascist song *Bella Ciao*. Spotify couldn't build you a more perfect resistance mix.

"Cold bev, Chris?" I ask the big guy.

He grabs it in a flash, his eyes still locked on the ground. I can sense his disbelief. I check one of my pockets, and I manage to find a vape that I place in front of his gaze. Mrs Patel smiles warmly for one second. Chris's eyes light up, and he inhales a strong vape as if his lungs depend on it. The exhale of relief brings the tension to a closure, for now. I gently rub Mrs Patel's shoulder.

"We'll get through this too, mate," I tell her.

·····

It's the day after, and many people have started taking the routes underground to their respective bases. We've been walking for an hour, and we are a few hundred yards of rail away from Hounslow West. What are we going to tell them? How long will the supplies last? Am I to blame for the loss of life by playing an important part in this rebellion that may have achieved nothing? Ultimately, it was me who sent that radio message two weeks ago. The echoes of the explosions still ring in my head, each one a reminder of a choice *I* made, a risk *I* took. I can close my eyes and see each hopeful face of those marching past me towards Westminster, then have that image replaced with their dead bodies a moment after.

Gerrard waits by the platform, perched on the edge, his legs dangling beneath. He looks at his gun as if inspecting it for the first time. He aims it loosely at a billboard for pension investments that boldly claims, "The future is here." When he spots us, he gets up giddy and grabs us in a hug. I never thought he had such a wingspan; it's as if he's stretching just for this moment.

"I'm so glad you guys are okay," he says while he checks us all physically like a mother seeing their child again after some time away. "You must be hungry; come eat!" Case in point.

As we sit down to eat some leftovers from their overnight dinner—some spaghetti and meatballs—more people flock to us. We are encircled now, and I feel like one of us must speak to break the tension. Their faces look down as if I need to confirm our defeat at Westminster. They need to hear it, to believe it. What they saw before the drones stopped streaming was not enough.

Both Chris and Mrs Patel slurp their spaghetti with an empty look on their faces. Around us, people glance at me, expecting me to tell them what happened. I clear my throat, but there's a lump there still.

"Look, everyone, we know as much as you do…" I say whilst trying to catch every look around me. "There were 20-odd explosions around us, and they weren't us, so…"

"So, Moss and MBGA are still there?" asks one of the people, his arms crossed in disbelief.

"I don't know. They might be, or this might just be a desperate last-man-standing attempt–whatever that might be."

There is silence and anticipation. They all look at each other, begging the other to ask another question. A few people nod and move away from us, disappointed. I wish I could offer them more.

Gerrard observes the whole discussion. I see him about to address the crowd, and I shudder at the thought. Who knows what wacky theory lies behind those eyes and between those ears?

"Listen," he says as he captures the group's attention, making a few people turn in their tracks. "Dom knows as much as we do. There is no point in launching theories now. We sit and wait, and hopefully the army will contact us once the situation clears up."

"Yeah, the army—they have planes in the skies," says one person, trying to emulate a glimmer of hope.

"And all the equipment they need to figure this out," says another.

Some contagious optimism seems to be taking over.

"Yes," continues Gerrard, "we have supplies, comms, and each other. This was our reality weeks ago, but we were alone and isolated. Now we're here, together. We made it through then, and we'll do so now."

I see a few nodding, their confidence increasing. As

a proud parent, I'm watching this nerd become a leader, calming people down. Patience echoes Gerrard's thoughts, trying to reassure people.

"Make sure you sleep in pairs. We'll set up some patrols," she says as she distributes some blankets.

I bite into a meatball, feeling that the situation may be just under control, and Gerrard is the best person to deal with it now. He draws the crowds away from us while Patience, done distributing blankets, brings us a plate of weeks-old baklava.

"Something sweet, for afters," she saysas she follows Gerrard and the crowd, helping people organise around the station. After all, she knows it inside out.

.....

It's almost a week before we hear anything new. The days drag by, a tense waiting game, with no word from the outside. Then, finally, soldiers appear at various tube stations, their presence almost surreal after the stillness of the days gone by. They move purposefully, letting everyone know that the outside was safe again, though that word seems to have lost some meaning.

I eventually meet Captain Fowler on a desolate Hounslow West High Street, a place that once bustled but now feels like the hollow shell of a city. The streets are eerily quiet, lined with crumbling facades and half-buried memories of what used to be. Fowler was overseeing the distribution of aid packages, directing soldiers like pieces on a chessboard.

"Dom—glad to see you, bud," he greets me, his voice a strange comfort in the chaos.

"You too, mate," I say, shaking his hand firmly, though my eyes can't help but drift to the wreckage around us. "So... what was all that?" I ask, hoping he could shed some light on the unfolding madness.

He exhales, rubbing his neck. "We don't know, I'm afraid. All we can tell is that it's unlikely to happen again. We've eliminated all the targets, and as far as our tech guys can figure out, it looks like some self-destruct mode was triggered when Moss was taken out. But honestly? Your guess is as good as mine."

His words land hard, but in a way, the idea of "unlikely" was the new normal. Far-fetched theories and uncertainty were no longer dismissed after what we'd been through. I scan the area, watching soldiers move supplies. People gather around aid trucks. The skyline looks like it has been chewed up and spit out by some cruel god, with smoke clouds moving from west to east.

"So, what happens now, Captain? Does the army

take over?" My voice sounds detached as if I were asking about the weather, yet deep down, I feel worried that we were exchanging one heavy-handed ruling for another.

"Temporarily, yes," he replies, his tone measured but with a touch of empathy. "Until we can be sure the enemy is fully dismantled and no longer a threat. We'll roll out plans like the ones we use for natural disasters. Keep people safe, restore order, that kind of thing."

I keep nodding, but I feel that Fowler could read my thoughts because he pauses and looks at me with a hint of disbelief. This wasn't the future we'd imagined—a people-led recovery, rebuilding from the ashes of tyranny. This felt... sterile. Controlled. The exact thing we had fought against.

"Look, Dom," Fowler adds, a little softer, "This is temporary. We've been fighting alongside you and are not about to turn into oppressors. The people will have a seat at the table. But right now, we need order. People need structure, or we're just inviting chaos back in."

I want to believe him, but the unease gnaws at me. "Are there no politicians left? Labour? Tories? Greens, anyone?" I ask, trying to wrap my head around how things would function without elected leadership. One thing they don't tell you about anarchy is that the rising sounds good on paper, but when the takeover is complete, there's a vacuum to be filled quickly.

Fowler shakes his head, looking grim. "As far as we know, they're all out of London. They must've cuddled up near some fireplace in some donor's estate. Most of the government fled when things went south. Seems like they see the city as too volatile."

"Can they do that?" The question felt almost rhetorical, but I need to ask it. I need to hear it aloud.

"If the last month taught us anything, Dom..." He trails off, but I don't need him to finish. We both know the answer. The rules have changed. Or maybe they no longer exist.

A superior officer calls Fowler over. He shakes my hand and walks down the street, leaving me amidst the debris and makeshift relief stations. My legs feel like they're making a considerable effort to keep me balanced, and a chill moves up and down my spine. I want to experience the joy of the win, but it feels far from that.

I stroll down the high street, scanning the area looking for signs of life and normalcy. Some shops had their blinds pulled halfway up, their owners peeking through cracks, cautiously testing the waters as though they weren't sure whether to hope or to hide. Gentrifier-favourited cafes that had previously sold avocado and sourdough toast had now turned to spam on rolls. No one was rushing to take aesthetic photos of that. I spot Gerrard and Patience huddling around a small table with a smoothie between them. They wave me over.

I join them, sliding into the seat next to Gerrard. He hands me the second half of the smoothie, the warmer half, and I sip it absently, still processing everything Fowler had said.

"So, Fowler says the army's sticking around for a while, but he swears it's only temporary. He thinks people need structure, but..."

I stop. They know what I was thinking.

Gerrard leans back in his chair, his brow furrowing. "Yeah, but temporary can easily become permanent if we're not careful. And 'structure' can turn into discipline real quick."

Patience nods, her face serious. "We don't distrust the army, Dom. But a military government? It's a slippery slope."

I sigh, leaning forward, my elbows on the table.

"Okay, hear me out," I say, my voice low. "We need to get ahead of this. If we don't want the army to become the new authority, we need to start organising now. We can't just be reactionary."

They both agree, but the weight of what lay ahead was pressing hard on our shoulders. People looked up to us now. And not too many were keen to follow the army blindly.

THE COMMUNE OF HOUNSLOW

The first sunny day of the spring season is upon us in the commune, with the characteristic British rain not holding us hostage anymore. The natural light fills the tent now and shines on my workstation. I'm hyper-focusing on my task—fixing our radio. *"What did she say? Red to Green or…?"* I think this is what they call ADHD. Can never seem to focus too much when Sophie's speaking to me; I always drift between her mouth and her eyes. I decide to chance it. It's a radio, what's the worst that can happen? A few buzzing noises start to emerge whilst I try to tune it finely.

"Good mor…. from the… cil of Lond…"

"Red to Yellow, Dom," she shouts as she lowers a crate of milk bottles by the entrance. "Right." And without trying to be smart but rather gracious in my lack of knowledge, I nod to her, as the radio shares the daily broadcast in a crisp transmission.

"Today, we celebrate the anniversary of our victory day. The army and the Council invite you all to the Peace Festival outside Buckingham Palace, where the London settlements will compete in a sports day, awaited by all, to be commenced with a music show by Adele and Coldplay, sending in their holograms from Europe, and a live set by our very own DJ NUKE."

"Is she still in Estonia?" I ask.

"Adele? Yeah, her place in Hampstead Heath is still squatted. That community is only growing bigger." She smiles at me and packs some things before she heads out.

She knows all the gossip of the town. Or the commune, rather. Sometimes, I wish I had that much capacity to give people the time to chat away. I've been heavily focused on maintaining some equilibrium here, and people see me as a leadership figure. Therefore, the less I speak, the more weight my words carry. Sophie is my opposite. A chatter and a yapper on all levels. She has such a natural way of connecting with people instantly, making everyone fall in love with her, and so did I when I met her. Almost in an instant. I remember how, during one of her first few days in the commune, I went out of my way to make some dessert for the commune's meal to sugar my way into her good books. I don't miss an opportunity to tease her and say that she only dates the kitchen custodian knowing she could always get that extra dessert.

"Oi, Dom are you around?" I hear Gerrard shouting from the outside, his voice growing louder as he approaches.

"Inside, you fool," I invite him, slightly annoyed, as I now have to turn down the volume just as DJ NUKE is about to play some garage music. Gerrard's head pops through the curtains with a grin. "Have some manners, will you? No need to shout." I reprimand him.

"Ah, shut up, mate, this isn't *Bridgerton*, my lord. And this isn't a palace; it's a tent. I can't even knock." He says as he taps the tent's tarp with his knuckles. "See? Keep your royal manners but grab your tools; I want to show you something."

I give in and step out of the tent following the frizzy-haired nerd who has become, ultimately, my best friend. Over the past year, we have worked side by side to build what is, with a hint of bias, the best commune in post-apocalyptic London. Our own little Garden of Eden. We walk along the main pathway, where Hounsies, the beloved residents of our commune, have put tens of tents together on one of the former golf links we have turned into a settlement.

There are a few houses that survived the fighting, scattered on the outskirts of the commune, but most people preferred the idea of simplicity and egalitarianism, living in tents and enjoying the shared buildings, like the mess hall or the kitchen. Our choice for developing a settlement mainly with tents was as much of a rejection of the former structure as a need for flexible and easily adaptable commune planning due to the ongoing influx of people.

About a thousand of us currently live here. Various similar settlements have popped up around London since, with people trying to build communities with their neighbours and participate in society differently than before. There are still settlements that follow older rules of societal structure, and we all meet at the Council weekly to participate in the collective society that is London.

"So, here's the thing. Remember how we struggled with that well earlier last month with insufficient depth," I nod. "Well…" I laugh briefly to appreciate the un. "Abu found a digger in a nearby yard. We need to fix some of its mechanics."

"Gerrard, you know I know fuck all about the mechanics of diggers," I say, stopping in the middle of the path feeling disturbed pointlessly. "I have some work to do in the tent, genuinely not in the mood for a useless stroll".

"I know, you silly man," he says as he pulls me by the arm. "But you have the tools, and we might need to do some lifting." He feels my arms and looks at me. "You know a thing or two about lifting, no?"

Reluctantly, I accept. Ultimately, that well is important to the commune, and the tools I have gathered meticulously over the past months might come in handy, finally. I always had a weird hoarding mentality when it came to tools; Sophie sometimes complains that there are too many hammers and screwdrivers on my bedside table. I never learned how to fix things, as no one taught me, but I always hoped that maybe that's how I'll fill my time in retirement. Unfortunately, that's far away from today. Despite not being glued to an office chair, every day is a day of work in the commune.

The path stretches almost a mile and connects everyone. I see Edna, the shopkeeper, dusting the outside of her tent with a fern-made broom.

"Afternoon Edna, how's things?" I say in passing.

"Alright mate, how about you?"

"Not too bad". That's what we fought for. The British small talk. We were closer than ever as a community, still as shallowly interested in each other's lives.

Edna was a Slavic immigrant of unknown origin who kept to herself. The last few years have really worn out her enthusiasm and dreams of a future in this country. In all our chats, I never got exactly where she was from. But she was a master of succinctness and a proficient small talker. To think people were saying these people do not assimilate. Edna was more British than me.

As we keep walking, I only just notice Gerrard is wearing some weird spandex shorts, the type that cyclists wear with a self-assuredness that I always envied.

"What's up with little Gerrard there?" I say, pointing at the shorts. "Why is he joining us today?"

He takes an innocent second to realise.

"Ah, yes, mate, I've signed up for cycling. I've missed the wind going against me!"

"Did Patience approve this outfit, or did she break up with you? Is this some act of coping or brevity?"

"Nothing like that, mate. It's just that with this gear, the aerodynamics are enhanced when you…"

...and I zoned out. Nothing unfamiliar between me and Gerrard. He always has an explanation, just a bit too lengthy for my liking. As he keeps babbling by my side, I notice Sophie speaking to one of the farmers, and I wave and smile at her. We carry on down the path to the construction yard, where Patience and Abu await.

"Sunny day, eh, whiteboy?" She greets me with a familiar warm smile.

"Ma'am," I nod as I lay my tools down and inspect the machinery with the conviction of a father who knows how to do it all but needs some time to analyse it from afar. You know the stance: hands on hips, check top to bottom, rest your chin in your chest to take it all in, inhale heavily, and hope somebody else picks up the work. Gerrard hugs Patience and kisses her whilst Abu approaches me.

"Dom, hand me the tools. There's a new lad in the commune who was a mechanic. I'll get him to help with the work on it, but I need you and Gerrard to prop this up so I can put a plank under a wheel. It's stuck in the mud, you see."

I saw. From my previous *fatherly stance*, I massage my chin and look around the digger to show proper consideration to the information given and analyse all the ways forward which I may or may not suggest.

"I agree. It seems stuck in the mud," I say, stating the obvious. "Let's get it on with it." So, we do.

Once we finish, I leave Abu the tools and wave goodbye to Patience and Gerrard as I return to the commune when I hear her from behind, "What's for dinner, Dom?"

"Fresh food, as always!" I reply, not willing to spoil the surprise.

·····

I count all the produce and write down my formula on a piece of paper. We have a lot of mouths to feed, and only today, another twenty-odd people have arrived from Richmond. I lift my head and see Sophie awaiting instructions, pen in hand.

"Sophie—get the cooking station prepped, please. How many volunteers do we have tonight?"

"On my way—10 in the kitchen and about 20 helping with delivery."

"Good, get the kitchen staff rounded up here when you get a chance. Thanks."

She nods and gets on with her task, diligently checking her notes and directing people to different stations. The kindness in her voice makes people oblige without question—she always rolls up her sleeves to help in the commune, so there's a lot of goodwill for her going around. One evening, during a tense situation in the mess hall, she stood between two Hounsies arguing over bin collection duties, addressing both with the assertiveness of a general, the logic of a professor and the empathy of a mother trying to calm egotistical toddlers. She turned frowns to smiles, fists to handshakes and tension to cooperation. A true mediator in that sense. Where was she before all this? We could've achieved our uprising much sooner with her voice leading us.

Lost in thought, following Sophie with my eyes, I see Mrs Patel approaching me, and I greet her with a smile.

"My dear," she says, "I think you are wearing yourself out here."

"What do you mean?"

"The size of this task is growing," she says, looking around the kitchen. "It made sense in the early days when there were a hundred people, but now?" She rests her hand on mine. "We need to come up with a better system."

I don't want to agree, but the tiredness of repeated cooking has caught up with me. Sure, we have plenty of volunteers each night, but I can't remember the last time

I had a proper night off.

I have always appreciated how Mrs Patel has a sixth sense when reading people. I could escape the interrogation of my worst enemies, be a traitor in that famous TV show we all used to love, and perhaps even lie to Sophie. But there is no escaping Mrs Patel's observations, underpinned by her deep care for those closest to her. Ever since losing Mr Patel, we have become her family, and her responsibility for keeping this family together is a role she takes seriously.

"You're right, but we can still make this work for now." She nods, but as always, is about to give me a moment of wisdom.

"Listen, give a man a fish—you know the drill—these people need to get back to being able to fend for themselves."

She pats a stool next to her, inviting me to sit down, and I oblige. She is shorter than me, and this is her way of telling me to sit down so she can run her hands through my hair and comfort me.

"People look up to you, which comes with a lot of responsibility. You can't be everywhere at once."

"I know," I say defensively. "But that's why Patience

is the leader, and we share responsibilities. You see Gerrard getting more involved too, Sophie…"

"But none of you asked for this. You helped create this place, but the Hounsies are grown-ups. At some point, you have to let go and trust them to live the values of this place." She invites me to stand up, raising her hand, which means the comforting session is over, and the truth is no longer sugar-coated.

"You have to trust others, Dom. You saw for yourself what happens when you try to control people."

She was right. I've been so involved in this project that I forgot to let go. The cooking club grew, and there are so many people here who can take over at any point. My reputation got to my head, and I felt the need to lead the commune's feeding efforts, but there's a difference between bossing and leading, and I forgot to do some of the latter. I started running this as a free-for-all restaurant, instead of a place for upskilling and growing a community.

"Perhaps I lost focus, being too involved from within," I admit, to her and myself. She smiles.

"Perhaps taking a few steps back will grant a better perspective?"

I nod and thank her for the pep talk. The kitchen staff walk in, and I step forward to greet them.

"Alright, Chefs, day 365. Are we ready?"

A chorus screams, "Yes, Chef."

I look at the front row, where Charlotte looks eager-eyed as always, her uniform impeccable and the grip on the wooden spoon as tight as a soldier's on a rifle.

"Charlotte,"

"Yes, Chef!" she says with a big smile.

"How about you run the show today?"

She nods and, without a second thought, turns to the rest of the volunteers whilst I take a step backwards next to Mrs Patel, who grabs me by the arm in reassurance.

"Main Course—I need Rodney, Kesha and Tina on the veggies. You two newcomers, with me on the soup. Dan and Mike are on dishes today. Let's go, folks; the mess hall is filling up." She commands with a perfect balance of authority and collegiality.

"Yes, Chef," the group responds enthusiastically.

BREAKING BREAD

The day of the *Peacefest* is upon us, and I wake up to a murmur outside my tent. I open my eyes to see Mango standing on my chest, pinning me down, his whiskers twitching ever so slightly.

"Mango, dude, what's up?"

"Meow. Bitch. Bad vibes," he says, using a paw to comb his fur.

"What bad vibes, dude? What are you on about?"

"Stay high—goodbye. Stay low—you get another go. Meow," and he jumps off the bed after dropping the most cryptic waffle on me. Lately, he's been acting weird; I hope he's not spending too much time with Gerrard listening to his wild theories.

I clear my eyes with the palms of my hands. Sophie is sleeping soundly to my left, her mouth slightly open, letting out the faintest of snores. I kiss her cheek, put on a shirt, and step outside.

The commune seems so lively, there are so many colourful outfits and people are smiling throughout. Edna brings a few crates of wine outside the shop and passes the bottles to people. I didn't think the festive atmosphere would take over, but I'm reminded that not everyone is a cynic like me. *Maybe this was an excellent idea, actually?* I try telling myself in an attempt to hijack my gut feeling. I see Patience braiding a young girl's hair, and I smile at her. She finishes it quickly and walks towards me.

"Dom, the digger is fixed. Abu said the mechanic offered to share the shift with him to dig the well."

"That's great news! Is there a Council meeting today before the festival?"

"It is, and I cannot make it. I promised I'd help Gerr with getting there and cheering him on from the frontlines, rather than a balcony. You know he needs a bit more coddling…"

"I get it," I reassure her. "Do you have someone to attend the meeting, or would you want me to be your deputy?" She smirks briefly and grabs my hand, almost pleading with me subtly.

"Would you, Dom?"

I nod in agreement.

Patience became the unelected matriarch of the commune very early on. She did not have to fight for her role or convince people. Her presence naturally tended to leadership, offering calm and solid judgment at times when passions or individual interests were high. In the early days, there were many times when the morale of the commune would take a hit. Who knew building a community is not as easy as assembling a certain Swedish-corporation-made drawer? There are no instructions for rebuilding community, and the pack does not come with all the tools and screws. She weathered us through the whole year, ensuring a level of community that neither I nor others would have achieved. Offering a lending hand in building, a well-timed hug when needed, and a voice for equal representation in our task distribution. She led by inspiring others rather than deciding for them, which made sure that she was not once questioned in her role, and I was happy to know that the commune was in good hands.

I walk back inside the tent and catch Sophie standing upright with her arms crossed. "Next time wake me up? I need to get ready, do my make-up…" Guilty as charged. Though I could never wake her up when she sleeps so peacefully. Fills my heart up.

"Sorry, Sophie. Look—I need to head to the Council today." I say, sorting through my shirts, looking for the *nice* one.

"Aw, but what about the parade? I thought we were going together?" Her hands join in front of her waist, and her gaze lowers. I get closer and gently lift her chin with my fingers.

"I'm sorry, I wanted to." I kiss her forehead and stroke her cheek gently. "Patience needs someone to take her place today, and she wants me."

She grunts for a second but accepts.

"I'll be with you right after the address, yeah? I'm not staying on the balcony like fucking royalty."

I hated the thought of being up there with all the other leaders. Some respected the responsibilities of their leadership, but there were many egos there that I did not want to mix with. Sophie knew my counsel to Patience would accompany the occasional *external* affairs duty. It's just a shame that it had to fall on *Peacefest*—we all looked forward to a little celebration, given we had actually managed to maintain some semblance of peace for a whole 365 days.

With a gentle smile, she gives me her blessing.

"Pass me that green dress, and away you go!" I pick up the dress from the makeshift clothing rack and hand it to her. "You're going to miss out on this!" She playfully places her dress in front of her body.

"I think I'll get the best view from up there!" I kiss her, grab myself a pair of shades to complement the outfit and make my way out of the tent.

·····

The bus is packed with festivalgoers, smooching couples and drunkards singing in the back. I find a seat by the window. En route to Buckingham, the streets are filled with people wearing colourful clothes. The roads cracked from the war make the journey slower than usual, however, the sun is shining through the row of buildings on both sides of the road, and all I can see are balloons, flags and smiles. Today feels festive, although I cannot stop a niggling thought that a sober atmosphere would be more appropriate. After all, we have lost so many of our own and so much of our former lives.

A massive street party has blocked the main road through Chiswick towards the city, so the bus diverts—I see smoke from grills and hear beer glasses smashed on the ground to the cheers of drinkers; it's almost as if the last year had not happened. It is beautiful and equally naïve how we can have such a short memory, like a protective mechanism for perpetual pain. It's also interesting to see how different settlements have chosen to live. Chiswick is a great example of something slightly resembling the past. Most houses are not damaged and shops have adapted to new requirements. It always had a flair for the "*have-a-lots*". Your usual leafy, suburban area of London. I guess it wasn't a priority for the fascists to tear down.

After about an hour of bus ride, I arrive at the Palace. Two military men scan me as I pass through the main gates, checking my pockets and running their hands across my body, looking for anything suspicious. I cannot help but feel uncomfortable. Whilst their uniforms are those of our peacekeepers, their stance and the control routine feel eerily authoritarian.

"Don't worry; I'm just a chef. If there's a knife anywhere, it's for dicing onions," I say, squirming.

The older army fellow stares me dead in the eyes, unflinching. "Good to go, funny guy."

Making my way up the stairs, I see Fowler, now one of the army representatives on the Council, greeting me from afar. He's chatting with that pompous douche known as the Duke of Primrose Hill. Spotting me, he salutes Fowler and departs.

"Dom!" says Fowler, extending his hand. "Are you here on cooking duties? The usual catering 'round here is rubbish."

"I'm afraid you're stuck with finger sandwiches, Cap," I respond jokingly. "What did that douche want?"

"Ah, just the casual pleading for emergency funding. They need more investment in puppy yoga and bullshit like that. The usual essential needs of the upper-middle class."

I laugh out loud, attracting some ungracious looks from the older military fella. I'm starting to think I got off on the wrong foot with him. Fowler gestures to follow him towards the Chambers. Away from the people making their way in, he pulls me slightly to the side.

"Dom, just to warn you, the situation is a bit tense. We have some intel of some radical resistance trying to disrupt today. The atmosphere might not be as friendly as the festival suggests."

He seems anxious, constantly looking over his shoulder, which is unusual for him, so I begin to wonder if he's not telling me everything.

"What radicals?" I whisper as Fowler makes a hush

gesture and invites me into the main room where the Council is about to begin.

I walk in, and as always, I'm struck by the excessive opulence of the Chambers. About fifty people were in what was once a royal room where they welcomed other royalty, heads of state, and celebrities. Claudia Winkleman, former TV host of a great show, *The Traitors*, and shampoo commercial specialist, is the only celebrity left, currently leading The Richmond Society. Packed with representatives of different settlements in London attempting some centralised peace-making, common good, and unity PR, the room is bustling today.

Everyone sends representatives for the interests of their people. Still, the army organises this Council in an attempt to bring people together and make London a city rather than a collection of settlements. So far, we have managed to get the transport up and running again, repair some critical infrastructure, and set up markets in all the boroughs where a distribution network sorts out food and supplies for each settlement on a needs basis. In that sense, we are pretty equal and united.

"Please help yourselves to our locally sourced sandwiches," shouts the master of ceremonies.

"Is it SPAM on rolls again?" asks a disgruntled voice.

"You can go a day without prosciutto, you pompous prick," another voice hidden in the crowd responds.

There are plenty of differences among us. Firstly, we are still separated from the rest of England, and different settlements have different views on the best way forward. Secondly, there are many ways in which different settlements contribute to the city's success. We often trade and try to help each other, but some, in the greedy fashion of our forefathers, prefer to keep to themselves. Tensions between settlements get to be discussed in these Chambers, and for all the faults of the army as an institution, they have managed to maintain peace and cooperation rather well. A few local, territorial fights have been well-tempered before flaring into broader conflicts.

The eyes of the crowd turn towards General MacArthur, who is taking a seat and clearing his throat to draw attention. His military past was evident in every sharp movement and barked command, as well as in the attention of the ranking officers surrounding him. When he speaks, the murmurs and side conversations immediately die down, a testament to the respect—or fear—he commands. His eyes appear borrowed, not fitting the rest of his image. They seem warm and inviting, betrayed by his stoic presence and rigidity of body language. The grey, neatly slicked back hair, without one solitary strand sticking out, was a testament to his military discipline, even reflected in his combing skills.

"ORDER!" he shouts, breaking the chambers' small chats. "First order of the Council—*Peacefest*—I assume all of you have sent representatives for the competitions?"

His voice boomed with the weight of someone who had led in times of crisis and recovery, leaving no room for hesitation. Looks of agreement amongst the group ensure we move to the second point of order, supplies.

"Now, a second item has been motioned by the Duke of Primrose Hill. Permission given to speak, Duke."

The tall, slender man rises and clears his throat.

"Ahem. Thank you, General and thank you, Council. I want to address the current distribution of supplies. We at Primrose Hill do not find this equitable. We have artists and thinkers; they need a certain amount of comfort to maintain some level of culture in what is now, evidently, a decaying city. We do not see the point of this *Piss*-fest when money could be better spent in the settlements that provide something for the cause." He pauses and stares directly at me.

"We do not wish to continue to subsidise settlements that like to play hippie-commies and live like savages while producing nothing for the advancement of the city." Some members of the audience groan.

I raise my hand to counterpoint.

"If the honourable douche…ahm Duke, would like to visit us in Hounslow. I promise to slap up a three-course meal that no overpriced café with 10 different almond milks can put together" Some giggles can be heard.

"I would rather eat a cold pastry at a lower league football match!" responds the Duke smugly, as a few laughs can be heard.

"ORDER" interrupts MacArthur. "Gentlemen, this sounds like a petty issue and a quarrel amongst you. Duke, your point is noted, but I feel that apart from a few cheap digs, you are yet to make a sustainable proposition. Do you have one?"

"I do not yet, General", he responds, slightly fidgety, "But I was hoping we could all discuss…" The general raises his hand, shutting the Duke down and taking over. "Then, may I suggest you draw up some plans, and at the next Council meeting, we will reopen conversations about the distribution of supplies?"

He lowers his gaze, disappointed.

"However," continues the General, "And I mean this bluntly—you must temper some of your expectations and remember to have balanced views. There are needs across the whole city, and not all can be met. Not currently." The Duke sighs and takes his seat.

"All in favour of listening to the Duke's plan at the next meeting?" concludes the General while an "Aye" can be heard unequivocally across the room.

"Good—today is about showing face and unity. *Peacefest* will kick off soon, and when I make the commencement speech, I want all of us to stand united on the balcony for everyone to see. We need to inspire community more than ever." We all applaud.

"Now—and this is a warning—my officers are informing me of certain radical movements growing across the capital. I advise you all to keep an eye out in your community. We do not want to feed the virus that got us here in the first place."

"But, sir," interrupts David of the Clapham Clan. "Are we in some sort of danger?"

The General exchanges some looks with his head of intelligence, who shakes his head anxiously.

"We can't assess at the moment. They seem to be working and moving clandestinely. We do not wish to become an oppressive force and spy, and control the population. Just be aware that violence can always breed again. If you sense any dangerous politics in your communities, bring them to the Council to discuss them and see if we can address them collectively before someone else does. Now… proceed to some canapés before we head out."

We start clearing the seats and head to the main room leading into the square. The Duke grabs my hand on his way out.

"Listen, Dominic. No hard feelings. Our ways of life are just incompatible. We have different needs."

I scan him from head to toe, and I am very aware that I could lift him and bang him against the wall. Something about him and his arrogance feeds whatever anger is left in me. However, I am in Patience's place today, so I choose diplomacy instead of caveman politics.

"Understood, mate. You have your needs, and I have mine." He smirks. "Concerning each other's needs, though, I need you to fuck off now."

His smirk fades. He huffs and puffs with posh theatricals and departs.

I grab a few salt and vinegar crisps and hold them in my palm. I walk around the room, gazing at the artwork. These royals sure lived a cosy life. I bet they're now somewhere in Scotland shooting badgers or something. I bet they never liked London, so I'm not surprised they didn't stick around to lead the recovery. That's hard work, the likes of which you can't delegate to servants.

I look around and feel like I'm with a group of squatters cosplaying the UN, having champagne from flutes, ready to address the masses of adorers. I don't enjoy what feels like a cultish element to this celebration, this photo-op on the balcony. Who are we kidding?

A year ago, most of us scraped for leftovers in filthy underground stations, dodging bombs sanctioned by elected officials. Now, some 16-year-old army intern is pouring me champagne until I say *"stop"*. It's funny how we resort to old habits each time we try to turn a page as a society. There must be leaders or a ruling class. Someone needs to wave at the masses from high up and shepherd them to prosperity or peace. This doesn't seem right, and I have an uncomfortable itch all over my skin.

Some bloke with a camera enters the room and directs us towards the balcony. As the doors open, the low sound of the masses becomes a full-on noise, with loud cheers across the square. These people seem genuinely happy to see us. We take positions in a seating arrangement that feels like the box of a theatre.

The general starts the festival with a quick address, and we watch the sports competitions. After running, up next is cycling. I felt like a posh estate owner watching the commoners sweat for a trophy. All I'm missing is a smoking pipe and a folding fan to push the smoke to one side, in total disregard for any non-smoker around me. Why would I care? I own land in this fantasy, and my biggest worry is the size of my tax bill. I scan the starting lineup and spot Gerrard in the most aerodynamic spandex suit and sharp shades. He salutes me as he does some unflattering squats.

One shot is heard.

For a brief second, I was about to duck my head and respond to danger. Thankfully, it's just the one that marks the start of the competition, but I couldn't shake my initial reaction. My palms are sweating, and my heart is beating slightly faster. The race is on, and they start cycling to the Mall. I scan the crowd one more time, hoping to see Sophie. It shouldn't be that hard. All I have to do is spot the dress that I bought for her at the Kensington market a few weeks back. Scanning the crowd, I end up seeing her, lifted on one of the boulders by the statue, waving at me. I wave back, smiling.

The crowd starts agitating around her. There are some screams, and people start rushing away. I can't tell what it is. I check around the people on the balcony, and they do not seem bothered, seemingly concerned with their bets on the cycling. In the commotion, I see Sophie slipping from the boulder and falling to the ground. I freeze, and the noise around me goes mute. For a moment, I can't move. My mind screams her name, but it's as if my body is disconnected, frozen in fear. My heart is pounding loudly in my ears. Then I'm moving—legs like lead but unstoppable—pushing my chair aside and stumbling on the stairs towards the main gate. As I approach the crowds, the commotion slowly returns, building and feeling deafening. Sounds of multiple gunshots can be heard among the screams.

Dodging people running in my direction, I manage to reach the statue and find Sophie on the ground with a bloodied head and motionless. I get on my knees and can feel her breath. I am focused on her as if the rest of the world doesn't exist, but I feel thousands of people running mindlessly around me, screaming and shouting.

"Soph, you okay? Wake up, please." I say, gently rubbing her shoulders.

She moves her eyelids slowly and seems to regain consciousness.

"Babe—are you okay? I heard gunshots."

"Uhm… yes, I think. I think I slipped…" She moves her hand across her forehead and spots the blood. "Is it bad?"

"Nothing some paracetamol can't fix," I say, trying to reassure her, but my heart feels like it's about to explode. I keep rubbing her shoulder in a bid to reassure her, but also to stop my hands from shaking.

As I cradle Sophie, my eyes drift to the chaos unfolding around us. Screams, gunfire, soldiers scrambling. A banner unfurls under the balcony, high above the palace gates. Bloodied and frozen in their seats, the Council members look like grotesque puppets trapped in a macabre display. Beneath the grim slogan, **THE ONLY WAY TO ACHIEVE PEACE IS BY TRUE SOCIAL ORDER**, a black pyramid looms, its apex illuminated like an unholy beacon.

Soldiers march toward the front gates, their guns raised, scanning the eerily deserted area. Each step echoes against the hollow silence left by the fleeing crowd. Crumpled flags, half-empty bottles, and deflated balloons all lie abandoned like remnants of a broken celebration. Cold and hard, the truth settles in my chest: this party is over.

THE HARVEST AT HAND

"Can't believe we missed hologram Adele," mumbles Gerrard as he bites into a piece of bread soaked in gravy. I give him a death stare and turn towards Patience. She seems unbothered or, perhaps, reflective.

"Patience, come on, say something." I urge her to as she turns to gaze across the field of growing wheat, where a few people are working the ground.

"Guys, take a break, please, it's rather hot. There's food by the kitchen and water from the well," she says as if giving them grace.

"Patience, I—"

She slams her fork on the table assertively.

"Dom, love, chill. We don't need to panic." There is calm in her voice, but I feel she is trying to mask her worries. "I'm aware of what happened. Fuck, the whole city is. Let a moment or so go by so people can catch a breath, and then we'll discuss."

She was right. My anxiety was at a high I've not felt in a long time. My hands have been clammy since I held Sophie in the middle of it all. After all, had it not been for her falling and hitting her head, I could've ended there and then. I've been staring at food without an appetite, and hearing Gerrard masticate irritates me.

"I would've won the race, you know", says Gerrard as he keeps chewing on that bread, his eyes empty.

"I know, baby," says Patience as she comforts him.

My body feels as if it's pricked by a thousand needles. I'm forcing myself to get up and do something as if stillness means succumbing to the uncomfortable. I leave my plate by the cleaning cart, returning to my tent. Jamie Foxx, the fox that followed Mango and the rest of us for the past year and found a life in the commune, is waiting by the cart, begging me for scraps. I throw him some leftovers.

"There you go, buddy. There's some meat left on this bone."

The walk home is sombre. I see Edna dusting her porch, as usual. She greets me in the correct British way.

"You alright?"

"Yeah. Y'alright?"

"Yeah."

"Edna," I say, stopping in my tracks, "Where are you from, mate? I never asked you."

She keeps dusting, avoiding eye contact, as if she does not want to reply.

"Aw, you know," she says, "lived a bit here, lived a bit there." She looks back at me. "You alright?" This time, it sounded like a concerned question.

"Yeah," I wanted to ask her a bit more, but I felt as if she was not interested in chatting, so I gave her a symbolic tip of the hat and carried on.

I continued my walk to the tent where Sophie had been resting and recovering from her fall. I find her inside, standing upright, head bandaged, and working on her laptop.

"Is it the slot now?" I ask, checking my watch.

"Yeah, come here; there's 15 minutes left, and the English news is covering it."

The "slot" was a one-hour satellite-powered internet access time across London. This rich man, Vylan Tusk, saw an opportunity to make some easy pounds by negotiating with the army when the internet infrastructure went down, and England did not want to help. To some,

Vylan Tusk is a genius and visionary; to others, he is just an opportunistic, silver spoon-fed privileged man with a robust, cultish personality about him. Often a fan of extremists and with a penchant for propagating disinformation, his monopolistic ownership of various infrastructures meant he was in pole position to benefit from yet another disaster. Regardless, this one-hour slot access means we can stay in touch with the rest of the world and keep ourselves out of the darkness and isolation that frequently define our experience.

"Look, Dom," she says as she reads the article's title. *"Half the Council of London shot dead or critically injured in a terrorist attack, with tens of victims…"* She scrolls past the title to the body of the article *"…the army wishes condolences to the victims' families and that the perpetrators have been neutralised… the death of the General and the rest of the Council members should help unite us in our common goal of getting London out of local politics and back to being a city proud amongst others in England."*

"Does it say anything about the group that did this?" She scrolls but can't find anything. There is, however, an article in "related news."

"Ok, here we go; *Who is behind the Pyramid,* okay, okay, ah, for fucks sake!"

"What?" I ask as I get closer to her.

"Fucking paywall."

I guess you can only get rid of capitalism so much before it creeps back in.

"Leave that for a second. How's your head, Sophie?" I ask while trying to remove her bandage to check.

"It's good; I still feel a bit of pain, but nothing too unbearable…" Before she finishes her update, her eyes move to the other side of the tent. "Aw, Mango! Hello, good sir!"

The sassy cat graciously walks into the tent, stopping mid-stroll to lick one paw.

"Meow. Meow. Bitches." He stares me in the eyes, blinks and turns away, stretching towards the entrance before departing with his tail erect.

I bring Sophie a glass of water, and before I can sit next to her, I hear some intense meowing outside the tent.

"I'm going to check on him."

The sun is gently setting, and it's getting late; soon, it will be dinnertime. If I learned one thing over the past year or so, it's that nothing can bring people together like a home-cooked meal, and maybe tonight I will pull something a bit more spectacular to really take people's minds off yesterday's events. I check the main road in the commune, and it seems deserted; there's a cool breeze making its way through the tents and buildings. I feel a tickle on my shin—it's Mango's tail.

"Meow. Follow bitch."

He leads me to the kitchen and gets on top of the main counter where I usually prepare my meats.

"What's up, mate? Do you want some chicken?"

"Pouch."

I conform and place some jelly meat on a plate for him to slurp. He gets it done in three bites, licks his whiskers and stares me in the soul again.

"Meow. Suspicion is like a hairball, bitch. It feels urgent and real, but in the end, it's mostly nonsense and spit. Meow." His whiskers tremble, and something catches his attention. Just as quickly, he darts outside through the crevices. Ever since I smoked that catnip with him in the *days of the unknown,* I've built some weird telepathic bond with Mango. He comes across as slightly philosophical and, to some degree, an extension of my consciousness. Sometimes I wonder if this is all some fever dream and I am actually in a coma, in a hospital in West London, where life is normal and the past year and a bit has not happened. I wonder if I've been sacked from my job for absence due to ill health and being unable to work remotely, as I am unconscious. My friends are probably doing online fundraisers to keep me on the ventilator, saying how much of a nice guy I am. Little do they know I use my ventilator time to fight imaginary fascism and smoke catnip with Mango. I wonder what got me into a coma in the first place?

The sound of many eager footsteps approaching brings me back to the present. Today's volunteers have shown up.

"Afternoon, all," I greet them. *Am I in a coma?* Still rings in my head.

"Afternoon, Chef," responds Charlotte, on behalf of them all. "We heard about Sophie. We wish her well."

"Thank you, Charlotte."

"Chef—this is Byron," she says as she's stretching her hand to announce this well-groomed, twenty-five-year-old-looking guy. "He's joined us with the Richmond group that arrived the other day. He heard about Sophie's absence, and offered to help tonight. We could use as many hands as we can."

I nod and extend my hand to shake his.

"It's a pleasure to meet you, Chef. News of your skills and kitchen know-how has travelled the land, and it's an honour to assist you tonight," he says, smiling in a star-struck manner.

"Good to have you, Byron. What made you leave Richmond if you don't mind me asking?"

He rubs the back of his neck, slightly embarrassed.

"It's Claudia, Chef." He lowers his eyes, "She's running Richmond Society a bit like the Traitors. They have banished some of us."

"Sad to hear that mate," I say, acknowledging his misfortune. "Welcome to Hounslow, though. I hope you're ready to get your hands busy."

He nods and seems eager to help. I turn back to the group.

"Okay, gang, people are hungry, sad, and need some hope. I suggest we cook something full of love that will combine nostalgia with that feeling of comfort. Tonight, it's cottage pie."

Cheers and encouragement follow, and we get to work. A few people are responsible for gravy, others for the veggies, two people make a few kilograms of mash, and Charlotte and three others prepare the mince. The smell of gravy is to die for. Walking around the stations, I see Byron struggling to dice the onions, so I try to check on him.

"Alright, lad, how's it going?"

"Chef, I'm sorry, I'm a bit slow—"

"Don't worry," I interrupt his apologies. "Look, you hold it here." I show him a good technique while offering him a rag to clean up the tears. "You've not done this much in Richmond, no?"

"Sorry, Chef, my parents weren't around much, and food was always a nice takeaway or a meal at a restaurant. For a brief period, we even had a chef living with us when mom was on a Keto diet and needed balanced meals."

"Must be nice having someone always cook you meals?"

"Yeah—I miss my old life," he says serenely. And I don't blame him, who wouldn't? "Anyway, thanks, Chef; I'll follow your instructions."

I smile and walk away. The prep gets done in less than 2 hours, and hundreds of boxes are ready to be delivered. In the aftermath of the apocalypse, when many companies left London, we ended up with an insufferable number of electric scooters per capita. Nonetheless, these previously demonic inventions are extremely useful now, when there are hundreds of tents or houses to reach with a warm meal in a small space. The deliveries run smoothly in a well-rehearsed and practised orchestrated effort, and people get fed.

Early on, Patience, Chris, Gerrard, Mrs Patel, and I agreed on a set of ground rules for the commune. The most important? Everyone contributes. Whether working the fields, cooking, delivering, teaching, or attending the markets, everyone plays a role, adapting as needed based on priorities, fitness, or mental health. Our community thrives on the principle that we're only as strong as our weakest link.

This system, while largely effective, isn't without challenges. Complaints occasionally arise about some not pulling their weight, and years of societal conditioning—*worthy vs. unworthy, hard workers vs. grifters*—are hard to undo. At times, I've wrestled with whether we need stricter rules or even punishments for those who seem to exploit our compassion. But I quickly dismiss those thoughts, reminding myself this isn't the system we want to replicate. There's no money or hierarchy here—your effort is your barter, and we're all in this together.

I grab a cart with a few dozen meals and go to the mess hall. Some of us like to eat together, including the volunteers and some commune members. It's usually a place where we get together for announcements or festive meals. Patience greets us as we walk in.

"I smell cottage pie, whiteboy!" she says with a big smile on her face.

It's funny how morale works. From walking in the kitchen earlier feeling sick and not hungry, to now being around the Hounsies, finding comfort in pie and community. People are passing the sides around the table. We savour our meal and find a few things to joke about. The atmosphere seems a bit more relaxed, at least on the surface.

"Knock-knock", says Gerrard.

"Who's there?" Sophie asks.

"Peas."

"Peas, who?" She insists.

He lifts a glass of wine, ready to toast.

"Peas to share this meal with you."

Patience rolls her eyes while Sophie chortles. I see Jamie Foxx's tail under the table, looking for scraps.

Bowie, Gerrard's cat, is right by him, trying to beat him to bits of the pie that do-gooders pass under the table. Mango is on one of the windowsills, just eating jelly-pouched meat and supervising the whole ordeal. This wine tastes deliciously crisp and fruity.

·····

I wake up to the sound of fussing in the kitchen. I hear glasses falling on the ground. It's right next to our tent, so all the noise can be heard. It sounds like rummaging. I want to get up, but I feel exhausted, my body pressed against the mattress. Sophie is snoring beside me, and one of her arms lies on my chest. If I move, I might wake her up.

The noise, fortunately, stops very quickly. Must've been Jamie Foxx looking for scraps.

·····

The following day, I wake up to Edna screaming outside my tent.

"Who was it? Which one of you?" she shouts, going around knocking on people's doors and tents.

I get up swiftly and go see what all the fuss is about. People start coming out of their tents, too. All of a sudden, we've got ourselves an impromptu town hall.

"Edna, Edna, calm down! What's up?" I ask, almost half asleep. I see Patience making her way down, too.

"Someone stole some of the meat I brought over last night," She says, holding up a ripped bag. "The kitchen is a mess."

I go inside with Patience to check the kitchen. There's not much damage, but indeed, some cuts of beef are missing.

"It's you and your posh boys!" I hear Edna shouting outside.

We rush back out to find Edna in full-on attack mode, wielding her broom like a medieval knight, jabbing it toward Byron and some of the newcomers. They shuffle backwards, wide-eyed and trying to dodge her swings, but Edna is relentless, jabbing the broom at anyone in arm's reach. The newcomers look like deer caught in headlights, unsure whether to run or beg for mercy.

Byron tries to plead with Edna. "Wasn't us! We were in our tent the whole night." Edna seems unmovable and keeps trying to poke Byron with her broom.

"I don't trust you lot at all," she says menacingly. "You only, take, take, take!"

Patience invites calm, trying to mediate this brewing conflict as more people gather around. "Edna, no accusations without proof, please." She says as Edna grabs her broom tightly and starts rolling up her sleeves, almost as if she is ready to go after Byron. Or anyone at this point.

Suddenly, Chris appears—*fully naked*, with nothing but a vape in his mouth. The entire group freezes in an instant. Silence, apart from the faint buzz of his vape as he drags from it. He walks toward Edna, utterly unfazed by the fact that every eye is now on him or that his 'assets' are on full display, bouncing slightly with each step.

He gets close enough to smell the frustration steaming off her. He walks around her in circles, measuring her from head to toe. Without a word, he grabs and snaps the broom right out of her hand. The crack of wood echoes sharply, and everyone flinches. A faint gasp is heard from the crowd.

"Stop." His voice is calm and assertive. He takes a long drag from his vape, letting the vapour billow out slowly and dramatically. "If it's your lot," he says, eyes flicking to the newcomers, "I'll make sure this broom gets to meet all of you." He raises an eyebrow, utterly unfazed by his exposed state, and the guys shake their heads wide-eyed, not daring even to blink or move their gaze any lower. They look like they've seen a ghost—or worse, a naked man threatening them with a snapped-off broomstick.

Chris looks like he's on the edge, proper loose now, and the unspoken rule of the internet comes to mind: *never fight a naked guy acting aggressively*. It's a line no one's brave enough to cross, not even Edna, still seething beside him.

"Good. Better not be." He tosses the broken broom handle and casually turns, strutting back toward his tent like it's just another Tuesday. As he walks away, he blows a thick cloud of vape steam behind him like some bizarre, naked dragon. He stops and turns mid-vapour.

"Dom, meet me in a few hours. We'll hit the market and get some more meat."

The tension deflates as soon as Chris disappears like air rushing out of a balloon. The people watching start to disperse, mumbling and returning to their tents. Edna is still glaring at the newcomers, who awkwardly start retreating, unsure whether to apologise or make a run for it. The quiet lingers, an aftershock of whatever that just was.

"You owe me a new broom," she says, pointing at

Byron.

"Drop it, Edna, please," I tell her before getting back to my tent.

The situation dies down, and I see Sophie trying to get up. I rush to the bed to offer her an arm to lean on as she seems to be struggling.

"What was all that?" she asks worriedly.

"Just a bit of tension," I tell her reassuringly.

Deep down, I felt this was speaking volumes about how everyone is really on edge despite appearances. I feel the palm of my hand between my index and thumb, rubbing gently, trying to ground myself as a feeling of unease slowly creeps in. We have succeeded for so long in trying to maintain harmony, but that balance was always precarious. The events of *Peacefest* have eroded some of the trust among us, and how can you blame our people for it? Who are these Black Pyramids, and could they be amongst us? Have we been too welcoming to people we don't really know? But then again, how could you know people without letting them in?

Sophie looks at me whilst I stare at my hand, deep in thought, and snaps her fingers in front of my eyes, waking me up from my trance.

"What's up?" she says playfully.

"Fancy going on a short morning walk, get those steps in?" I say, trying to deflect from speaking my mind.

She smiles, and we go through the commune to the river. The Thames looks rather clean today, and you can even see fish. With no more bankers in the City, the levels of cocaine in the river have reduced, or at least that's what ecologists think. I wonder if the fish appreciate the newfound clarity of mind or if they're going through withdrawals, missing the stimulation.

Walking by the bank, we pass by many boats with nomads living in them. They belong to no settlement and live on the river, peacefully and isolated, fishing and growing tiny herbs on the boat's sole. The fresh air helps clear my head, but my stomach is still in knots. As we're slowly approaching what is the Brentford settlement, I see an old figure with a crusty beard sitting on a fold-up chair on a ragged boat holding what appears to be a gun.

He stands up and shouts towards us threateningly, "You. Turn around. Now."

I look around, and it's only us. There is an awkward silence in this part of the town. You can only hear the birds and the faint sound of traffic. Sophie is gently pulling my hand to let me know she wants to return. I freeze, staring at the man. Glancing away briefly, I spot a black pyramid on the starboard.

"Are you deaf or dumb, young lad?" he asks as he uses his gun to bang the side of the boat.

Suddenly, there's some chatter, and a few people start walking out of the boat, making their way towards us. There are three of them, wearing all black, relatively well-built and threatening in presence.

I lift my hands in a defensive stance.

"Apologies, sir, we'll be on our way," I say as I pull Sophie back.

Every few steps further, I turn around to see if we are being followed, and I can spot the men getting back inside. Sophie is gripping my hand tightly. I can tell she is afraid.

"It's ok, Sophie," I try to reassure her.

"Should we tell the others? Inform the Council, maybe?"

"I'll try to reach Fowler," I say rather quickly, betraying whatever confidence I wanted to portray. We find a fallen tree trunk and we decide to rest for a second.

"Dom, I think we really need to start asking questions in the commune." She says with a determined voice. "I know you want to see the best in people, but there are too many signs to ignore that some trouble is brewing. Maybe people have heard stuff?"

I sip some water from my reusable flask, staring into the distance. I was slowly coming to the realisation that there was merit to Sophie's concerns and, ultimately, Edna's too.

"I'm not saying turn Hounslow into Guantanamo Bay," she says, taking my hand between hers. "But maybe, keep an eye on things, behaviours, thoughts…"

"Police state, huh?" I interrupt her rather aggressively.

She lowers her gaze and watches the tips of her shoes tap dancing on the ground.

"Are you willing to protect your ideals or your people?" she asks, her eyes not moving from the ground.

I stand up and look around, letting her words resonate with me for a second. The trees are blooming, and the grass is green—somehow, life still thrives in the ruins of London. You can protect nature from man, but sometimes, nature's enemy ends up being nature itself.

You can scrub and polish a house all you want, but damp still seeps through the cracks, and mould still finds a way to grow. To not accept that is to not accept nature. If the universe, the grandest creation of all, is built on chaos and imperfection, how can I expect my community to be different?

"You're right," I say, lending her a hand and inviting her to join me on the rest of the walk home. "We need to be ready for what may come."

·····

The market is buzzing. New treaties that the army negotiated with European countries seem to have brought in an abundance of products, and stalls look fuller every week. Ignore the missiles, the fascists and the up-and-coming radicals; if you close your eyes, it could almost feel like the London of years ago.

"Ayo Chris, come check this!"

He departs the vape booth with a bag full and joins me at the vegetable stall.

"Wow, are these…artichokes?" he asks ignorantly.

"Yes, my friend, let's grab a few. I have an idea for the cook club."

"They look alien, these things," he concludes after a

close inspection.

"But they taste both earthly and heavenly at the same time," I say as I pick a few from the shopkeeper.

"Three fifty, lad."

We still use money, but its value is volatile. We try to follow the rest of England, but without a central bank, supply dictates the price. We pool some money each week in the commune towards the weekly shop, and the rest we grow ourselves.

With our community being diverse, we have plenty of immigrants or children of, raised with the idea that you should keep cash stashed away always. This worked out tremendously in our favour, unlike the crypto bros.

As we make our way through the market, securing all sorts of goods and supplies for the commune, the city is oddly brought back to life. A pub is full of people enjoying a cold pint, some religious folk are trying to get people back to churches or mosques, and people are angry at slow walkers— the picturesque, unbreakable, British society.

"Forgot to take a leak, Dom. Hold this for me," he says as he passes me the odd bags he was responsible for. Waiting around, my legs feel tired, so I sit on a bench and observe the world around me. I love the market. It's a nostalgic moment for me. Not to mention, I'm in my element here. Seeing fresh produce inspires me and gives me more ideas for the club. For several people at the club, fish and chips and maybe a curry was as adventurous as it got in the kitchen. Now, they're going to work with an artichoke.

A breeze rolls through, carrying the scent of sizzling food and spices, momentarily masking the stale air that still lingers in parts of the city.

That's when I feel it. Not see. Not hear. Feel.

A figure moves close enough that I catch the faintest whiff of unwashed cloth. No eye contact. No hesitation. A piece of paper is pressed into my palm quickly, almost unnoticeably. The man doesn't stop walking. Doesn't even turn his head. Just whispers a sharp, deliberate *"shh"* and disappears into the moving crowd. My stomach tightens.

I glance at the folded paper, its edges smudged, like it's been passed through many hands. My fingers hesitate before unfolding it.

Are You Tired Of Sharing The Fruits Of Your Labour With Scroungers?

The question stares back at me, printed in bold letters. Below it, a call to action:

Join The Movement For A Society That Works For Those Who Work.

And at the bottom, no address, no names—just a single black pyramid symbol, sketched in thick ink.

A cold weight settles in my gut. The edges of the flyer feel rough against my fingertips, but I realise I've been gripping it too tightly, crumpling it.

I exhale slowly. Calm. Don't react. Just slide it into my pocket like it's nothing.

They're here. In the market. Among us. Recruiting.

I scan the crowd, forcing myself to look casual, but my vision sharpens, picking up every face that looks too composed, every movement that seems too deliberate.

For the first time in a while, the market doesn't feel like home.

Chris suddenly reappears, oblivious to my rigid posture. He's got something hidden behind his back, grinning like an idiot.

"Here we go, Dom," he says, revealing… a leek. "For that soup later."

It takes me a second to process the joke. I exhale sharply—half a laugh, half an attempt to break the tension in my chest.

"Idiot," I mutter, shaking my head, the flyer still crumpled in my pocket.

"Let's bounce."

We make our way to the commune, and the wooden gates with the sign above welcome us. Chris stops to admire it as he takes a few inhales from his vape.

"What a beautiful sight. Can you believe it's been almost a year?" he says proudly.

I couldn't. In some ways, it felt like yesterday. As I stare at the wooden gates, nostalgic, I feel the flyer in my pocket again.

"I need to talk to you later, Chris," I say with a grave tone.

His lips press into a thin line as if he already knows whatever I'm about to say isn't good news. He nods. We step through the gates, welcomed by Sophie and Charlotte, their faces bright with excitement over our haul. But as Sophie pulls me into a hug, I catch something.

Her smile doesn't quite reach her eyes.

"YESTERDAY"

"What about the golf course?" said Patience as she handed me the map. "We can set up here by that former gym. There are a few empty houses, too."

I grabbed a pen and drew a perimeter around the Hounslow West golf course as Gerrard and Chris joined us from meeting with Captain Fowler.

"It's a go, guys," said Chris. "We can get a dozen."

In the early days after Westminster, some people returned to their houses, and others had nothing to return to, so they chose to relocate or leave London. About twenty-odd people who stuck with us at Hounslow West underground decided to join what we came back to propose as the *Commune of Hounslow*. In this settlement, we work for the common good, building a community away from centralised government, where we try to grow our crops, make our food, and live in peace.

Chris huffed, tossing the last tent pole to the ground.

"Right, that's it—no more fucking tents." He wiped the sweat from his forehead. "Why couldn't we have settled in a nice, abandoned hotel?"

"Because we're not squatters," Patience shot back, hands on hips. "We're building something different here."

I snorted. "Says the woman claiming a maisonette for herself."

We would use some of the deserted houses as more secure living spaces, but primarily, the goal was to live with as little as needed for a minimum of comfort. We were peaceful settlers, using freely available resources. We didn't aim to push the population out but rather invite others in. We didn't seek to take property or space that wasn't ours or was being offered.

The early days of building the settlement were tough as most of us had few ideas about what we were doing. Chris had some engineering experience and coordinated everyone else as a site manager. I decided to set a tent next to a derelict takeaway with a large enough kitchen to use as a workshop for my ideas, and having offered to feed the commune as my primary contribution, no one questioned it. Patience and Gerrard decided to take a small maisonette at the end of the road, designed to connect all the living arrangements. Central to our location was a former gym hall of a school, which we ultimately designated as a mess hall and a place where all of us could gather. We left ample green space to use for both recreation and harvesting. We would start small, with vegetables and fruits that we could grow, grains and herbs, whilst having a regular rota of people going to the early markets to secure other essentials.

The first meal in the mess hall was a memorable one. Until then, whilst working together, people were primarily concerned with setting up their living arrangements. Once that was done, the first dinner together was a marquee moment in organising our rules of governance. Mrs Patel and I cooked a Tikka Masala curry for the twenty-odd mouths to feed, and the smell of fresh naans in the room was to die for. I looked at Patience as we were all expecting some opening speech, and naturally, we all turned towards her.

She grabbed a naan and turned towards Gerrard, lifting it between them. Silence.

A quiet, heavy moment stretched across the room. All eyes landed on the naan, as if waiting for something unseen to take shape.

Then, without a word, Gerrard tore it in half.

"Today is the first of many when we live for all of us rather than just ourselves," Patience said.

We all nodded, and a few "*hear, hear*s" could be heard. Although she had a flair for the dramatic, her words were always inspiringly calculated, and her presence was respected.

"Share a naan with the one next to you and remember that we are in this together as one, for the best of all."

We were breaking bread. What a way to land an idiom, Patience. Kudos. The meal continued in silence, reflecting on the past week's events. We felt secure, but only just. We felt peace, but none of us knew for how long. Back then, feeling it at that moment was good enough.

A few weeks passed, and families or couples started arriving and enquiring about joining our commune, some travelling from other areas. Distributing housing and resources felt administrative, but ultimately, our goal was to build a strong, resilient community. And we needed as many people with good intentions as we could find.

Patience was sorting through the market haul one

winter day with a few Hounsies when a group of new arrivals entered the mess hall. Among them strolled an old man, propped up by a wooden crutch and a young blonde woman supporting his other arm. I walked over to greet them like a good host.

"Afternoon, folks; how can I help?"

The woman avoided eye contact, checking her surroundings almost suspiciously. The old man held her hand and told us their story.

"Our home on Chancey Road has been damaged since the events." Bill's voice was hoarse, his breath uneven. He took a shallow inhale before continuing, gripping his crutch tighter. "The water damage... the mould... It's on the walls. I have asthma, you see."

He coughed, a deep, wracking sound. The young woman flinched beside him, her fingers tightening around his arm.

I nodded, the weight of his words sinking in. Like him, there were hundreds of thousands in this city, all searching for a place to call home again.

"You are welcome here for as long as you need," I said without a second thought.

His daughter, Sophie, sighed in relief, lifted her gaze,

and flickered a small, hesitant smile across her lips like sunlight breaking through heavy clouds.

"I will put whatever skills I have to good use," she said. "My father is ill, so I cannot contribute as much as I need to look after him, but I will do anything humanly possible to support everyone's efforts."

I smiled. Before even mentioning our values as a commune, she already embodied many of them. I liked that.

"How do you feel about working in a kitchen?" I asked, feeling Patience's stare and whispers of "*white boy*" under her breath as if she was telling me off.

She hesitated, looking between me and her father. "I...I used to love cooking."

"Good. You're about to again," I said, trying to keep my tone light. "Kitchen's that way. You can perhaps help me out with lunch?"

She looked in the kitchen's direction, where a few people were already working. Her chin lifted as she saw some commune members working together to distribute supplies. When her father turned towards her with a smile and a glimmer of hope in his eyes, she told him, "We'll be good da," kissing his forehead.

My heart was growing, and my stomach was in knots.

Part of me knew that lunch was approaching; another part just remembered that feeling that I'd been drowning since the early days of meeting Yasmin. Something was magnetic about her. Through all the troubles she went through, Sophie was glowing. That initial moment of insecurity, when she arrived, was replaced rapidly by a fierce determination to provide care for her father. It made me want to care for her in return.

Patience observed our interaction the whole time. She came up next to me and hit me with the broom over my ankles from behind, extending her hand to greet our new guests.

"I'm Patience. Welcome to the Commune of Hounslow."

"Bill," says the old man. "Thank you for your hospitality."

The fresh herbs added a new dimension of flavour to the dish. It's so beautiful when you start chopping them, and that fresh flavour goes up your nostrils as if the earth is trying to seduce you. I chopped them as finely as possible and waited for the soup to be almost done. A trick I learned is always to add the herbs last; it gives the most impactful flavour. The lunch menu was simple since the city had a shortage of supplies due to disagreements among the communes. A vegetable soup served with warm bread. Mango supervised the ordeal and was sitting curled up on top of a high-up shelf.

"Do you need more help here, or should I set up the hall?" Sophie asked, checking on me.

"All good here—please and thank you!" She grabbed a few plates beside me and accidentally rubbed her hand against mine, muttering a shy apology with a smile.

Her smile was infectious. I turned around to the simmering pot and felt redness in my cheeks. Mango was staring at me, unimpressed.

"Meow. Bitch. You in love."

I instinctively went defensive,"Uhm, no, man, she is just a great help; I needed that," I said, avoiding his stare. I felt hotter. It must've been the steam from the soup. "I don't see you lending a paw to help."

He stared at his paws and started licking them, pausing just long enough to drop some more unsolicited wisdom. "Meow. Listen bitch. She good girl. Don't mess around, or I pee on your bed. Meow." And with that word of warning and his cleaned paws, he was off, and so was I to feed everyone.

·····

It was a few weeks before I finally asked Sophie out. We went on a few dates where we found we had a lot in common. We both hated the same things, which strengthened the bond. I remember how one day we were discussing serving brunch in the commune.

"And in no fucking way will we serve a sourdough bread slice that's hard as a rock," she said. "Who thought cutting a slice of bread with a knife and fork was the essence of comfort?" I was falling in love with her—she got it.

One night, I made a puppet show for her in my tent. I asked her to shine a light on one side of it, and I would be outside making all sorts of figures. Hearing the giggles from the tent was endearing. She liked small stuff, and to me, making someone laugh with simple things was something I hadn't experienced in a while. Another day, we were cooking together, and whilst I was mixing dough and she was stirring a soup, our free hands were intertwined. Mango was observing and made barfing sounds to voice his disapproval at our displays of affection, but we didn't care.

After her father sadly succumbed to his illness, I asked her to live with me in the tent and take our relationship to the next level. She needed some support and comfort for a few days, and I felt I could provide that. Taking her around my catch-ups with my friends helped her feel more included and protected. Mrs Patel took a particular liking to her, and Sophie felt a maternal bond with her. Mrs Patel would take her on errands, teach her some Indian recipes and talk to her about her life story and how, alongside Mr Patel, they built a life in this country. Sophie was a romantic, so she would eat those stories up, and for me, it was good to know that she had others to help her not feel alone in this new world.

·····

Six months down the line, the Commune was thriving. Around a couple hundred of us were here, from all walks of life, and more were joining each week. We were the perfect corporate "work with us" presentation page: a mix of ethnicities, sexualities, and social classes, all united under the belief that our differences can help us become a better unit. There was social tension at times, of course, as no human is perfect. For the most part, however, no one was above all, and that was a message that was wholeheartedly accepted.

One particular evening, about forty new people arrived. The mess hall had never been as busy as it was that night, and cleaning it afterwards was a task and a half.

"I swear, half these new arrivals think we're some sort of charity," Edna muttered, scrubbing a table. "I saw one bloke ask if we had an espresso machine."

"Maybe we should ration more strictly," suggested one of the original members of the commune.

Patience shook her head. "We're not turning people away. We figure out a better system."

"At this rate, we need a new system every week," said Edna, throwing a few glasses in a cart rather audibly.

I stayed silent, staring at the half-eaten meals left on the table. Across the room, two Hounsies exchanged a glance, their shoulders tense. One of the newcomers, a young man I hadn't seen before, pocketed an extra bread roll when he thought no one was looking.

It wasn't the first time I'd heard complaints. And it wouldn't be the last.

FRUIT ROTS FROM THE INSIDE

It's good to be back in the commune. The trip to the market proved bountiful, and I am very excited to use these artichokes. But before getting to the exciting part, I need to share this flyer with others—this Black Pyramids paraphernalia is ever-present, and I cannot shake this feeling of concern. It might be paranoia, but the language seems awfully similar to what MBGA was broadcasting in the early days. A reminder that fascism comes knocking at the door first, it doesn't just barge in.

Charlotte and Sophie help us with the bags as we take them to the kitchen. I see a few volunteers preparing some soup bases, and I greet them. I offer the bag of artichokes to Sam, one of the volunteers, and ask him to clean them for later. Patience and Gerrard visit the kitchen, and they are excited to check the haul.

"It's great to have you here," I say as I realise my inner confidants are all in the same room. "Follow me to the supply room, please." I grab Sophie by the hand and raise an eyebrow towards Chris, asking him to join us.

We start unpacking some supplies when Chris decides to open a bottle of wine.

"It's 5 PM somewhere!" he says, grinning.

"It's actually 5 PM here," Sophie notifies him while handling a glass. "You guys have been gone for a while."

Gerrard pops his head in and spots the wine.

"Aw, yes, love me a secret meeting with wine."

"Sit your arse down," I tell him playfully. Patience turns on an old radio as DJ Nuke is playing some jazz. The scatty jazz rhythm and the clandestine vibe of the meeting seem like the perfect setting to address my concerns. I take one sip of wine, swooshing it around to moisten every space of my dry mouth.

"Uhm, I need to speak with you all," I say. Patience lowers the volume.

As I tell everyone about our encounter with the people by the river, Sophie lowers her gaze, as if still shaken by it.

"And then, today at the market…" I say, showing them the flyer.

Patience picks it up in haste, eager to read it.

"*…works for those who work*," she says, shaking her head in disapproval "Where have we heard that nonsense before?" She passes the leaflet to Gerrard, and he scrutinises it, holding it against the lightbulb as if checking for hidden clues.

"Look," I continue, "All I'm saying is that we need to be vigilant. We don't know how big or small their following is. All I know is that there are a few blokes having meetings down the river."

"So what do you suggest we do?" asks Gerrard, passing the flyer to Chris who quickly glances at it before crumpling it in his palm and throwing it on the floor.

"Observe," he interjects. "As far as we know, they might have nothing to do with us, just with the centralised Council structures. They want to change minds, so they need minds to change." He takes a long drag of the vape, and the silence of our expectations fills up the air alongside the vapour. "Look—all I'm saying is this. We carry on as normal but watch who we let in the commune and what kind of talk happens."

"So—like an authoritarian state?" interjects Gerrard, his leg twitching.

"No—I mean—we need just to keep an eye out. If we hear or see something, we let each other know."

"Aw, so now we're some omnipresent leaders—" continues to rebut Gerrard.

"I've got a feeling you do not estimate the danger correctly, Gerrard", says Chris.

"No—fuck this, Chris." He says, stumping the floor and grabbing his glass in haste, "I think you do not estimate the danger this behaviour poses."

He takes a sip and makes his way out, but twirls, turning to us, to add more.

"Just look at Edna this morning. Then, look at the people ready to join her and point fingers without a shred of evidence. If we walk on the path of distrust, everything we have built crumbles."

He places the glass on the shelf and leaves. The thing is, trust is fragile. It takes one crack for the whole structure to fall apart. We've been through so much together, and yet, paranoia is creeping in, threatening to undo everything we've bled for. Chris sees that, and part of me does, too. He's pragmatic; in times like these, pragmatism can mean survival. It's easy to talk about principles when you're safe, but if your back is against the wall and you've seen what desperation can do to people… that's when practicality becomes your lifeline.

There is an awkward silence as we ponder what Gerrard just said. There is still jazz playing in the background, just loud enough to fill the blank left by his departure. I agree with the principles, but the practicality of Chris's suggestion trumps for me. After all, can we not do both? Maintain trust while being wary? The problem is, once you start down that road, questioning everyone and doubting their motives, you don't know where it ends. At what point does self-preservation become paranoia? Where's the line between protecting what we've built and becoming the very thing we're trying to resist?

"Ok," I say as I take my last sip. "Not much else to say now, I just wanted to let you know."

I can see Sophie and Chris staring down awkwardly while Patience smiles and nods reassuringly.

"I'll see you in the mess hall," I say, leaving my empty glass on the table. "We have a nice noodle soup for everyone tonight and some artichoke-based dish that I haven't figured out yet, so I need to be in the kitchen."

As I open the door, I hear Chris clearing his throat.

"Ahm, Dom,"

I turn.

"Yes?"

"Keep an eye out on that Byron boy, will you?"

I nod and make my way out as my shift is about to start. *Byron...* he didn't do anything to raise suspicions for me, but he seems to be on people's minds. I wonder if it's a pack mentality or something deeper I can't see yet.

·····

As I stir the stock and add some spices, I feel Sophie standing behind me. She puts her hand over my shoulder, and soon, her head rests against it.

"You know this will all sort itself out," she says, as if she could sense my worry.

I smile, but can't shake the feeling that the air felt heavier today. In more than a year since we've known each other, we have rarely had significant disagreements. Most of the time, we find common ground, and most of the time, I help find it. This time, however, I'm torn. Can one achieve freedom without security? What if security comes at the price of freedom?

Over at the vegetable table, I see Byron chopping some onions amateurishly. He spots me staring at him and raises his eyebrows as if seeking approval. I keep looking at him whilst stirring my soup, and I catch myself trying to observe his every move. Chris's words have got to me. He seems a simple lad trying to make do, but today, I see him in a different light. Is he that much of an amateur, or is he playing a bigger game here? Why does he not cry when chopping onions? Not a single tear. Is that enough for me to be suspicious?

"All good, boss?" he asks, trying to break the awkward moment.

I shake my head and smile back at him.

"Yeah—just overthinking. Help me take these pots to the mess hall?"

The tables are full, and I see little groups of people passionately discussing and advancing each other's theories. There are many hands covering mouths and whispering on the sides. The liveliness of the room is replaced by what feels like a game of Chinese whispers. Most avoid eye contact with me and tend to keep their conversations within the boundaries of their small groups. I look at Patience and raise my eyebrows, shrugging my shoulders. She stands up and taps a wine glass to draw everyone's attention.

"I know there is loads to discuss. I know we all have strong feelings. But I also know this soup will be delicious and cold by the time we end debating. Please, let's eat."

The bowls are filling up, and the sound of chewing and approving grunts fills the large hall. While some people are still enjoying their food, I see Chris standing on the other side of the table.

"Listen up!" He shouts as his voice cuts through all the noise. "The threat of the Black Pyramid is real, and it's no help denying that or burying our heads in the sand. If you know of a threat in the military, you take steps to pre-empt and defend. This we need to do."

A murmur of approval dominates the room. Patience looks towards me, and I raise my shoulders, unsure of what to do next.

"There may be spies among us—agents of political influence who want to take you to the days of before. The days when they benefited at your expense instead of sitting at the table with you."

I look around and see a few uncomfortable faces. Byron looks down at his bowl. At our table, I see Gerrard clenching his teeth and Patience's hand slowly caressing his back. His jaw is tense, and he avoids looking in Chris's direction.

"To those of you who are Pyramid believers, I tell you—leave. You are not welcome here, and your message of division will not be tolerated. I encourage anyone who hears such disgusting drivel to come to me directly, as I'll handle it." He bangs his fist on the table, but it doesn't feel authoritarian. If anything, it feels as if he's ready to deal with the situation. I, for one, do not.

Cheers erupt, and Chris sits down, smiling at us. Gerrard takes his bowl and heads to the kitchen.

"That's how you do it," whispers Chris to us. "You let them know you're watching them."

I look at Byron again. He doesn't join the cheers.

As the meal draws to an end, Gerrard is waiting for me in the kitchen with his arms crossed.

"This is not right, Dom. We're slowly giving away our principles." He looks worried. I want to reassure him, but I feel a bit powerless. Perhaps, to some degree, I agree with Chris.

"I don't know, Ger," I say, shrugging my shoulders. "If I'm honest, I'm a bit afraid of their rise, too."

He shakes his head, visibly disappointed in me.

"This is a slippery slope. You know what happens when people start turning on each other, Dom. We're next."

I don't say anything and watch him walk out of the kitchen, still shaking his head. Maybe he is right, but I lack a better alternative, and I feel responsible for the people, not my ideals.

I leave some dishes in the sink, and as I'm preparing to go, I can't help but spot Byron scrubbing hard on the pots.

"Lad—you helped cooking—that's it, head home and get some rest." He stops and turns towards me.

"Dom, I need this. I need to put in extra work."

"What do you mean?" I ask inconspicuously.

"You heard Chris. There's already doubt seeded, and this morning with Edna didn't help." He sighs and looks me straight in the eyes. "I want to be here. I want to prove myself." I pat him on the shoulder and nod, respecting his wish. "Appreciate you trying, Byron. We'll figure this out."

He smiles and resumes his scrubbing whilst I hang the chef's hat up.

In the tent, I see Sophie waiting for me into bed with Mango at her feet. I get in and get close to her as she makes room for a cuddle. We get under the blankets and start making out, kicking Mango by mistake.

"Hiss, Bitch," he mutters as he gets off.

I start feeling Sophie all over her soft skin, and for a brief moment, we get lost in each other with no concern for the world. As my lips move down on her abdomen, I stop.

"You smell that?" I ask. "Smells like Blue Raspberry?"

"Like wha—"

"Hello!" says Chris as he pops his head through the tent curtains.

"Motherfu—" I say, jumping under the cover to hide my naked arse whilst Sophie drags the whole blanket up to her chin.

"Relax, lad, nothing I've'nt seen before." Reassures us, Chris. "Look, I have a plan I need to speak to you about."

I stare at him angrily, asking if he couldn't have waited until the morning.

"Nope—" he assures me as he takes another drag of his Blue Razz vape. "We need to go now."

"Go where, you lunatic?"

"To the river. The boats. Time to do some spying ourselves," he says with a large, oddly creepy smile. Something tells me he loved this ordeal; it activated something in him that was lost since retirement.

Sophie manages to convince me it might not be such a bad idea since we don't know much about this faction. As Chris puts it, it is better to know what you're fighting rather than who.

"I mean, do we really want to be unable to walk around freely just because they say so?" she pleaded, arguing that I should go with Chris. I should've said no. I should've told Chris to put down the vape and get some sleep. But the truth was... I wanted to know. I grab a shirt in a hurry, kiss her goodbye and make my way out. Before I leave, I feel a paw on my forehead. It was Mango, sitting on his shelf by the side of the entry.

"Meow bitch, a fruit rots from inside out," he says as

he sharpens his claws playfully yet painfully on my forehead. "Build bigger tables, not bigger walls." And he jumps, leaving the tent and joining Jamie Foxx as he's screeching maniacally by the wheat fields.

In a cloud of Blue Razz vapour, I step out.

"Let's do some spy shit," I say, passing a flashlight to an eager Chris, who's ready to rock and roll.

"Show the way."

UNDERCOVER GRAINS

The rain is pouring down now, making this moment feel more *espionage-esque*. My city trainers were not equipped for this muddy environment. I can imagine Sophie telling me off when I return. *"What kind of idiot takes white trainers on a rainy day through the woods?"* I chuckle to myself. I always proudly wore my idiot badge.

I think there is a certain bliss in admitting you are an idiot. Society teaches us, or at least it used to, that mediocrity is shameful. You have to achieve at all costs. Each hour when you are unproductive, someone else takes your place in the queue to reap the rewards of meritocracy. You not only have to better yourself, you have to be better than your peers. Engaged in a perpetual race with your neighbours, you may be distracted by the burden of existence and feel you might have a shot at the world's riches. This illusion has kept the world going for so long that we have forgotten to question its premise. The moment I accepted I was mediocre, I discovered some form of happiness. Shame it took an apocalypse to teach me that.

Each step on the moist ground adds more mud to my soles. I move slowly, feeling the earth sliding under my feet and fear planting my face in it. With his military background, Chris moves like a feline. He ducks and crouches behind tree trunks as if playing Call of Duty. You can tell he misses a part of this, like taking an old dog for a walk on his favourite path.

The moon radiates through the tall oak trees, and the sound of rain dropping against the leaves is eerily poetic. The cold air sends gentle shivers across my arms, and I can see my breath before my eyes. I look around and can't seem to spot anything; Chris points to the east, where some movement shakes the bushes. The rustling is getting louder, and without a warning, we see Jamie Foxx jumping in our path, giving us a stare and moving in the opposite direction. Soon after, we see Mango and Bowie, following his direction.

"Idiots!" I say, breathing a sigh of relief.

He remains focused and unflinching, using a few hand gestures to direct me as if I'm a member of his Special Ops unit. I shrug, not understanding.

"There?" I ask.

He nods and hurries me up by pushing me from behind. Based on some of the war movies I have seen, I move amateurishly, but I feel like a fool. A few yards beyond the bushes lies the river, where Sophie and I saw the boat the other night. He pulls out a makeshift telescope and scans the area.

"Looks clear," he says, nodding as he inspects the boat. "I'll go first and whistle if you're good to come."

I trust the expert on this one, and he makes his way to the boat. I don't move, and I watch him stealthily approach the water. His feline moves turn into rolls and zig-zags from one bush to another. A bit further to my right, Mango and Bowie are staring at him too, equally impressed. There's a tap on my shoulder, and my heart is in my throat.

"Mate," says a hushed, recognisable voice.

I turn around to see Gerrard with makeup under his eyes like he's about to go hunting for deer.

"Ah, for fucks sake, Gerr, what are you doing here?" I whisper loudly.

"Just thought you might need backup," he says, holding a pair of hedge shears.

I see Chris waving and whistling from the boat. I turn to Gerrard, "Go back, mate; there's no need for three of us," I tell him as I make my way to the boat, trying to emulate Chris's tactical movement. Looking back, I cannot see Gerrard. Either he left, or his camouflage is working. *Impressive stuff.*

I step onto the boat and can feel it moving gently on the water. I'm not a fan of this, but I can't even claim sea sickness as we're in the shallow waters of the river. I just like the ground I'm stepping on to be still.

Chris opens the door to the boat, and as we walk in, we realise neither of us brought flashlights. Some spies we are. It is pitch black, and we can't see a thing. He taps me on the shoulder, and I look at him vaping. His device is one of those that lights up at the bottom when you drag it out. *Incredible*. He looks like a right fool with his lips sucking on that thing and wide-eyed. Two or three inhales around the room later, he finds the switch, and we have light.

The cabin looks inconspicuous in the clouds of vapour at first. A large map of London is tacked to the wall, with specific areas circled in red. Most circles focus on the wealthier districts—Mayfair, Kensington, and Chelsea. Next to the map, there's a series of Polaroids pinned up, showing various members of the commune, including Sophie and me, taken at odd angles. A chill runs through my spine as I look at these photos and realise they are quite recent. I pick one up and feel a tension in my wrist—there's one with us by the digger, just the other day.

Chris points to a half-open drawer. He pulls it out, revealing a neatly organised set of files. He flips through one and stops at a document titled *Project Phalanx*. It's filled with coded language and technical diagrams, but one phrase stands out. *Resource Reallocation Strategy*. Chris looks up at me, his eyes cold. Behind him, there is an odd wooden wall.

"Look," I say as I point towards what looks like a partition.

He pulls the wall away without much effort. Inside, there are some gas masks and a few rifles. We hear pebbles smashing against the boat's wood as we look at each other. I look out the window to see Gerrard making signs from the bushes.

"Chris, I think we need to go," I say as he inspects the newfound storage space.

"Chris—" I try again, but he seems hypnotised.

Outside, some voices can be heard. We freeze, hoping they will pass. We cannot make out what they are saying; the sound is muffled.

"Can you stop that for a second?" I whisper, slightly irritated.

Steps can be heard on the boat now, and the thing moves again slightly, making me nauseous. Chris slowly grabs a gun and starts pointing it towards the entrance. The door opens slightly, and a man's voice can be heard from behind.

"Gentlemen, I know you are here and have a gun drawn. Shall we take a few breathers and talk things through?" says a rather grave, posh voice.

I look at Chris; he seems unswayed and grips the trigger even more tightly.

"How about no?" he replies, "Why don't you just show your face, weasel, and then we can see if it's worth taking a breather?" The man kisses his teeth and opens the door. "Tsk tsk, Chris. You know nothing about us. Why so aggressive?" he says as he approaches ominously. A slender figure and a clean-shaven face appear. A tie with a Windsor knot and a vest underneath a jacket that looks expensive complement his outfit.

"Listen, Chris," he continues. "If you do not lay down your weapon, I have a couple of gentlemen outside with their eyes and scopes on a frizzy red-head in the bushes.

I look out the window, and Gerrard is in the same spot, watching it all, unaware that he has been spotted.

"Terrible camouflage," adds the man, to whom I reluctantly nod.

"Who are you?" asks Chris, slowly reducing his grip on the gun.

"Very well," he says as he grabs a chair, turning it around and resting his chest against the back of it on the opposite side of the cabin. I can spot a big baldy goon waiting outside the door, behind him. "The name is Sir Burlington. I am a knight of the Black Pyramid."

Chris lowers the gun slightly, but his gaze remains suspicious.

"We've got questions."

"By all means," Burlington says, folding his hands on top of the backrest of the chair. "But let's keep this civil, shall we?" Chris glances at me, and I agree.

"Fine," Chris says. "We'll start with the obvious—what are you people planning? And don't tell me it's just community outreach. We found the rifles, the gas masks. And what's this *'Resource Reallocation Strategy'* all about?"

Burlington raises an eyebrow. "Ah, quite a few questions! I see you've been thorough in your investigation. The *'Resource Reallocation Strategy'* is simply about optimising the distribution of resources across London. In times of rebuilding, we must ensure that those who contribute the most are adequately supported. It's about fairness, you see."

"Fairness?" I angrily ask, reminiscing about what brought the city to its knees a year ago. "By hoarding wealth in certain districts and leaving the rest to fend for themselves?"

"Not hoarding, no," Burlington corrects smoothly. "Prioritising. Those who have proven their capabilities—those who can rebuild society—must be given the tools to do so. Otherwise, we all fall together."

"So—you're ultimately MBGA," I say, frustrated. "And who gave you this responsibility?"

"No—MBGA was a fascist project. We are…an orderly project. A meritocratic one." He grabs a cigarette and lights it. "As for the responsibility, when this city is ready, we want to be too."

Chris narrows his eyes. "And the gas masks? The weapons? Is this how you're gonna get the city ready? By getting it to submit to your views?"

"Defensive measures," Burlington says without missing a beat. "We live in uncertain times, as I'm sure you're aware. Not everyone sees the Black Pyramid's vision for a renewed London. Some would prefer chaos, some want us gone, and we must be prepared."

"And what about the Council assassination?" I ask, unable to hold back. "We've heard the rumours. Were you behind it?"

Burlington sighs deeply. "The assassination was a tragedy—one that we do not condone. But the Black Pyramid is a movement, not a monolith. Some act independently, driven by misguided interpretations of our goals. We cannot control every action of every member, but we can assure you that the leadership does not advocate violence."

Chris scoffs. "Convenient. So you're saying it's just a few bad apples? What about this boat? What about these files and the surveillance photos? You expect us to believe you're just here to make the world a better place?"

He takes a few more drags of his cigarette, not losing

eye contact with us for one beat. It's almost as if he's disciplined in confidently engaging an audience. Like someone who makes money solely from motivational speeches to impressionable audiences.

"We have various areas we observe, for lack of a better word. The Commune is a great example of what happens when order is brought in, and people contribute fairly. If anything, we admire you folks."

"And the…"

"The pictures—yes. It's the folks we think are influencers. The ones we want to reach out to—build bridges, that sorta thing." Chris and I share a look. Me? An influencer? I want to feel flattered, but there's this niggling thought that I'm being buttered up to serve a darker purpose. I shrug my shoulders, but they're tight. My mind wants me to relax, but my body says no. Chris hands the gun to Burlington.

We still have many questions but feel bamboozled by the eloquence of his speech. It's as if he has an answer to anything. One you want to hear rather than a truthful one.

"Excellent. Now, I have a favour to ask. But first, fancy a cider?" he says with an ominous smile. "Oh, and your mate from the bushes can join, too!"

We both accept, and I look out the window to wave at Gerrard to join us. He shakes his head, disappointed and heads back into the bushes towards the commune. Burlington nods to the goon, and he pulls a box of ciders from a compartment in the hull. We each grab one, and feel a bit more relaxed. Chris is measuring Burlington.

"So, what's your story, then? Where were you when the events happened?"

Burlington takes a sip and looks away as if reminiscing.

"I was out of London that week. I had a business meeting and was caught up on the motorway the first night. Then," he stops and takes a sip, almost mimicking a tear, "I got a call from my father telling me about it all."

I look at him suspiciously. As far as I remember, the phone signals were all off. I try to hide my suspicions; for now, he seems like an open book, willing to share.

"What did you do?" I ask.

"Took refuge in a motel by the service stations. I was back from a business meeting with a cabinet member. I had many discussions with the government about the necessity of certain 'preparatory measures' in case of conflict, given all the talk of war." He takes a deep breath, "Who would've thought that war was just around the corner, eh? Once the explosions stopped, I made my way back to Chelsea."

"So what? Were you some sort of war strategist or what?" asks Chris.

"But how could you get through London?" I add, pressing on my suspicions. "There was green gas everywhere?"

Burlington seems unshaken by the barrage of questions.

"Well, I owned a defence company, you see; pass me that, will you?" he points towards the gas mask. Chris hands one over. He pulls a care label that has the inscription **Burlington & Sons** on it. "Had a few of these with me for demos. When I returned to Chelsea, I went straight to the warehouse and helped distribute masks to neighbours and friends. I thought I may not be able to save everyone, but I can at least help those around me. If you remember, the MBGA government was preparing itself for war, so business was good; therefore, I had loads of stock. Enough to help my area."

Convenient, I think to myself, but it all checked out.

And he didn't flinch once. Is he what he says he is, then? Is he a neighbourhood hero or a profiteer? Or maybe he is none of those. He comes across as forward. Pure? I'm not convinced. Guilty? Can't tell. We take a break from our questioning and sip the cold cider. The orange flavour really does trick my brain into relaxing more, or it might just be Burlington's suitable explanation. After all, his goons are around, and he's happily answering our interrogation when he could just as easily take a different approach.

"My turn to ask for something now, gentlemen."

We listen carefully as Burlington asks us to invite him to the mess hall so he can address the commune. The Black Pyramids sense that an election will be called at the next Council meeting and want to garner a stronger following with the help of the *influencers* they have identified. Or spied upon. They just want to share their vision of a unified, *meritocratic* city, as Burlington calls it.

Chris doesn't seem to have an answer, and I'm torn between the threat that such messaging might pose to the commune and the principles of free speech we hold. After all, why shouldn't they be heard? Will censoring them give them more of a victim complex and, in turn, boost their support? Is it worth having our people turned by their fancy meritocracy and order messaging? And if they are turned, were they our people in the first place?

"Fine," I say, "But on one condition."

Burlington extends his hand, waiting to hear my request.

"No recruitment," I say, but my voice doesn't sound as sure as I'd like. "One speech. That's it." Burlington nods, almost like he expected it. Like he knew I'd say yes. He keeps his hand extended, waiting for a handshake. I hesitate, but then…what choice do I have?

We leave cordially, and we'll see Burlington in a couple of nights' time in our mess hall. I'm nervous about how the commune will respond, but I have to trust that our community was built on strong foundations that a well-rehearsed, propaganda-type speech cannot sway.

On our way back, Chris is unusually quiet.

"You okay, mate?" I ask, trying to get him to share.

"You know what's scariest, Dom?" he finally says, exhaling slowly. "For a second there, I wanted to believe him." I nod and see where he's coming from.

"It feels weird," he adds.

"How so?"

He stops in his tracks and looks around.

"Like, I've been manipulated."

I agree. Burlington's charismatic nature and the subliminal threat of all eyes on us made us perhaps more susceptible to compromise.

"Look, Chris. I know it's not ideal, but we are a welcoming commune. And we always said that behaviours should be policed, not ideas." I say, trying to rationalise the fact that we agreed to give what we felt were dangerous ideas a platform.

"Yeah, but… are we sure they are what they say they are? I can't shake the feeling that we've been here before, and we all know where it led. D'you know what I mean?"

"I do," I respond promptly. "And at the same time, it's only a speech. I think it's important for us to see how the commune reacts to it."

He stops again.

"What do you mean, Dom?"

"Follow me here," I say as I take the vape from his hand and take a drag myself. "If our people, which are mostly victims of MBGA, resonate with what Burlington is saying and cannot smell the bullshit, then they were never our people."

"But what if they get fooled, though? The guy is very eloquent and to a degree… likeable."

"Eloquent he is," I agree, and pass him the vape back. "But we need agency moving forward, Chris. We cannot spoon-feed our people ideals and politics. Ultimately, we can only hope they can tell a wolf in sheep's clothing."

The meows of Mango ring yet again in my head. I feel responsible for my people, but should I feel responsible for their thoughts, too? I trust them to work for the good of the commune, but what happens when that purpose is presented differently? There is palpable tension already, and doubts have already been sown between some of us. Crossroads await us.

We arrive at Hounslow, and Gerrard is waiting by the gates with his arms crossed.

"You two are fucking idiots. Drinking cider with the fascists."

"Calm down." I say to him as he starts pacing up and down the pathway, repeating, "Cider with the fascists; I can't believe it."

"Gerrard—bud, hold on a second," says Chris firmly

but friendly as he grabs him by the shoulder.

We explain everything to him, and you can see his anger rising, making his cheeks red. I tell him about my thinking and why this was inevitable.

"If we maintain our values of freedom and openness, we allow people to choose rather than be corrupted behind our backs," I add.

"You're playing a dangerous game, Dom." He shakes his head, disappointed, and rests the shears by the gate before making his way to the house. It's almost 2 AM, and the commune is soundly asleep. I agree with Chris that we'll reconvene the next day with Patience, too.

I walk towards my tent and see Mango waiting for me outside the tent entrance in a loaf position, paws underneath and his whiskers straightened,

"Hey boy, what's up?" I greet him.

"Meow bitch. A chameleon changes its colours to blend in with the environment it hunts in." He turns on his back, spreads his legs, and starts cleaning his groin for two seconds in silence before staring back at me. "But ultimately, it's still a chameleon on a hunt. Meow."

He gives himself one more lick before sprinting unprompted into the kitchen.

I am too tired to track him now, and all I want is to rest next to Sophie. I am on breakfast duty, and that starts in a few hours. I land headfirst in the bed and I'm out like a light.

·····

I'm back in my old house, and the sirens are as loud as if ringing inside my kitchen. I step outside on the street, where I see Gerrard building a brick wall outside his house. I wave towards him, but he ignores me and starts to move faster and add more bricks, slowly disappearing behind it.

A limousine drives down our street and stops in front of my house. The window in the passenger seat goes down, and a man with a gas mask tells me to get in. I accept, and he waves the driver to go ahead. Once he pulls the window up, he removes his gas mask. It's Burlington.

"Dom, good of you to join. The air was dangerous there," he says, his voice smooth yet unnerving.

"Where are we going?"

"The Burlington & Sons factory, of course. I have a

proposition for you."

The limousine is pristine and smells like it's recently been deep cleaned. The leather squeaks at every movement.

As we drive through London, the tinted windows obscure the world, making it feel like we're in a bubble of safety. Inside, I sense anything but. Explosions feel muffled as if they are remote from us. The sound of relaxing jazz in the car makes it feel like we're protected from the trouble, flying above the city rather than driving through it.

"What kind of proposition?" I ask, confused.

"We need you to help us rebuild London. People trust you," he says with a smile.

.....

The radio wakes me up, and Sophie is playing with the frequencies. I keep my eyes closed as I'm still very tired, my head is pounding, and I believe the cider might've played a role in me acquiring this hangover.

"The Council will… next Monday to… the army suggests… change."

"Sophie, can you turn that down, please?" I say half-asleep.

"Sorry," she says as she gets up by the edge of the bed. "There are talks in the commune about some important Council meeting, and I wanted to see if there's some info on it."

I shrug my shoulders. I'm not sure what Burlington has in mind, and the last thing I want is to create panic and rumours.

"How was last night?" she asks as she gently moves her hand across my hair.

"I think I've done something bad," I say, getting up from the bed slowly. "Only time will tell."

A SEAT AT THE TABLE

As I crack a few eggs and whisk them in a big bowl to make an omelette, I see Mrs Patel walking into the kitchen. She puts on an apron and picks up a box off the floor.

"What's with you getting up so early? I heard you return late last night, " she says, picking vegetables from the box.

"I couldn't really sleep," I add a bit of salt and keep mixing.

She observes me and I notice it, but keep my sight on the mixing bowl, beating the eggs.

"What's on your mind?" she asks, laying her hand on my face and forcing me to look her in the eyes.

I tell her about the previous night and Burlington, my troubles reconciling what the Black Pyramids stand for and my doubts about their true colours. She listens closely, but I can see she is worried. Why wouldn't she be? She witnessed the rise of MBGA and was a direct victim of their rhetoric long before the bombs.

"Who's to say they're any different than those before them?" she questions, visibly concerned.

I struggled with the same thought, and it's no wonder those closest to me seem equally worried.

"I don't know Mrs Patel. What would you do?" I set the bowl down and give her my undivided attention.

"Rohan thought the same," she said, teary. "No one would flinch at his loyalty to the royal family. He would not dare question their motives even when they fled the country in the early days."

She picks some spinach and starts separating the leaves.

"Even when they graffitied the shop. Looted. Threw shit up our window. He always used to say: *The King will not let this country turn to hate.*" She laughs. "Poor old bastard. Always blind to the world around him."

I join her in laughter. We both miss him dearly. He was her world, and they had travelled the world together to this forsaken place to start their lives all those decades ago. I give her a hand with the spinach, but she stops me.

"Dom, for the past year, you have proven yourself

over and over. In everyone's eyes as well as your own."

She places her hand on my head. "This," she says, moving her hand over my chest, "is just as important as this. Trust your instincts."

I smile and can hear some noise outside. More volunteers start arriving, and she hugs me before returning to washing spinach.

"I remember the early days, Dom," she says softly, her hands pausing over the spinach. "It always starts with small, reasonable requests. Be careful with how much you give them. Sometimes, even a little is too much." She carries on with the spinach before sensing her words may worry me further. "However, I know you will do the right thing at the right time."

When is the right time? I keep thinking, whisking mindlessly until those eggs are begging me to stop. *What if the right time has passed already?*

Even this delicious omelette cannot temper the tension in the mess hall. As I eat, I watch groups of people talk to each other, covering their mouths. I look at Gerrard; he eats peacefully, somehow pleased with himself.

"Oi!" I whisper at him whilst throwing the end of a baguette in his direction. He raises his eyebrows.

"Have you started spreading the word about you know who?"

He shrugs his shoulders and eats the bread. With a mouthful, he replies.

"The sooner they know, the sooner they can make their minds up. I'm not going to hide this from our people. Will you?" He looks smug as if trying to test me.

I roll my eyes and scan the room again. The tension is evident, and, to some degree, suspicion has taken over our usual morning excitement about the day ahead. Some Hounsies drink their milk without touching the food. There is a lot of whispering and groups gathering in tighter circles. It's as if everyone is guarding their closest. Friends and thoughts alike.

I raise and clink a glass to draw people's attention.

"Guys—word has spread faster than my intention allowed it. Let's address it then in the spirit of trust."

Their eyes are wide open, following me. A few last clatterings of forks on the tables lead to silence.

"Yes, Chris and I went to the river last night, where we came across some members from the Black Pyramid." The murmurs in the room start intensifying. "Let us assure you that we are as sceptical as you are," I was looking at Chris for support, but his head was down, focused on the eggs on his plate. I turn to the crowd. "If they are indeed what we are afraid they might be, it is better to know them now. Keep your friends close and your enemies closer, you see? It is just a meal and a speech, nothing more."

"They are terrorists!" says one voice from the hall, supported by some affirmative cheers.

"MBGA reloaded!" says another, to chants of many "Aye's".

Patience stands up, and all the charged energy tones down as quickly as it grew.

"Folks," she says, trying so graciously to meet all the eyes looking at her. "Let us not forget who is asking for some diplomacy here." She points towards me. "The food you eat, the roof above your head, the friendship throughout—this man." A few smaller agreeing noises are starting to be heard.

"Now, like you and Dom, I have my fears about this—but remember, do not confuse hospitality with endorsement. For us, it is a simple decision: allow them to speak in front of everyone or behind our backs, cracking the foundations of this commune. If we are as strong as we believe, their words shall ring empty, and we will strengthen our principles further." Some scattered applause can be heard.

"Tomorrow, let's be on our best behaviour. We listen, and we move on. I do not want tension or violence. Those who try anything against this will be banished. We will look out to make sure things run safely." She concludes as she nods towards me.

The murmurs seem to end in agreement. The mess hall slowly returns to its usual rhythm, but the air is thick with anticipation. The Black Pyramids will speak tomorrow, and the weight of their words could tip the balance of everything we've fought to rebuild. I sense my right hand shaking, but before I can hide it under the table, Sophie places her warm hand on top of mine.

After the intense discussion in the mess hall, I return to the tent, my mind still churning with doubts and worries about the Black Pyramids' visit tomorrow. As I step inside, I find Sophie browsing the internet.

"Is it our slot?"

She nods. "Just checking a bit more on these Black Pyramids. You see, there is this Council meeting on Monday?"

"Yeah, I think there are talks of elections," I say as I

lie down in bed, staring into the nothing of our tent ceiling. She notices me and stops her browsing, joining me in bed.

"You look exhausted," Sophie says softly, brushing a strand of hair away from my forehead. "Come here." She gently pulls me down so my head rests in her lap. I close my eyes, letting her fingers run through my hair, the motion soothing in a way that feels like, for just a moment, I can let go of everything.

We sit silently for a while, the only sounds being the distant murmurs of the commune setting about their days and the soft rustling of the tent in the wind. It's peaceful—a moment to forget about the storm brewing outside, if only for a little while.

"I talked to Mrs. Patel this morning," I finally say, my voice barely above a whisper. "She's worried, Sophie. She's seen this thing before, and she's scared it's happening all over again."

Sophie's hand pauses for a second. "I know. It's hard not to worry about everything that's going on. But you're not alone in this. We're all in this together. Whatever happens, we'll face it as a community, as a family."

For once, her words hit as hard as a punch in the gut. My stomach feels twisted, and there's an overwhelming feeling of dread raising each hair on my body. *Family.* I open my eyes and look up at her. "What if I'm making the wrong decision? What if letting them speak gives them more power?"

She gets up and extends a hand. "Follow me," she says as she drags me out of the tent.

We stand outside the kitchen. Inside, a few volunteers are cleaning dishes. Upon noticing us, they greet us with a smile.

"You see this?" she whispers, waving at them. "You didn't build this alone, but it was your vision. We all work together here now."

I loved the kitchen, and I loved how each volunteer treated it. From makeshift sandwiches to elaborate meals, we've done it all in the space of a year. What started as Mrs Patel and me working hours on end to feed all the refugees was now a well-oiled machine, giving people both food and purpose.

I didn't even notice Sophie leaving me as I was stuck in place, looking at the volunteers. "Come on, let's go further," she shouts from afar. I rush my step to catch up with her. We walk past Edna as she is cleaning the pathway to the shop.

"Y'all right, Edna?"

"Yeah, you?"

"Yeah!"

We end up outside the wheat fields. "How about this, Dom? Could you have done all of this by yourself?" I shake my head. I was just an account manager before this. The closest I've been to a farm was buying organic eggs at the market. Luckily, we had a few sons and daughters of farmers who helped prep the soil and made sure it had all the nutrients needed to thrive. I pick up an ear of corn and can't help but be proud of all its kernels, as if they were mine.

"Cool—one last spot," Sophie says, dragging me gently by the collar of my shirt like a dog on a leash.

Our long, slow walk takes most of the day. We chat about the past, the future, and, more importantly, the present; the only place I never seemed to really live in. She has this wonderful gift of grounding me. All that time, people used to spend on meditation apps and videos to relieve their anxiety, when Sophie was all we needed. But Sophie was not unique; she represented a deep connection I had yearned for so long. A place of comfort, where only the present mattered because the way it felt was irreplaceable.

At the end of the commune, a small hill from the former golf course rises slowly. *Hole 17 Hill*, as we called it around the commune. Young couples have date nights there, and children use sleighs from the top when we have some bouts of snow. It was a landmark of the commune. We walk up and stop at the peak, a few feet above the ground, when Sophie asks me to turn around and check out the commune in all its glory, with the sun setting gently in front of us. It looks picture-perfect, and the sun's last rays dawn beautifully over the tents and fields.

"Now this Dom—this is all of us. Not just you. You are not responsible for every soul here. You have to give them agency and allow them to make up their minds and hearts. Got to let them stay or go if swayed."

I pondered her words for a second.

"What are you trying to say with all of this, Soph?"

For some reason, I need it spelt out. I never set out to be responsible for every *Hounsie*, nor have I expected them to think and act alike. If people look up to me, I can only share my view, not enforce it. I can only guide, not tell.

"I'm saying," she grabs my hand between hers and looks me in the eyes. "You are right in trusting these people. This—"she says, looking at the commune in its sun-blissed light, "This couldn't have been without trust. You can't protect people from the big, bad world. Protect them from harm, not from their own thoughts. Let their moral compass guide them."

"So… you're not worried?" I say, feeling a bit more reassured. "All this could be flying Black Pyramid flags soon, back in the old system of *rags-to-riches* fantasies…"

"Of course, I am worried. But not worried for you, for us. Worried about the state of this city and their popularity." She pulls out a small bottle of scotch from her bag that seems to have been hidden, only to be brought out for this special moment, this place, *the present*. "Should they want flags with that symbol, let them set them outside the commune." She takes a sip of the scotch before passing it to me. "And if there's any among us that buy into their propaganda, would you rather not know and see it with your own eyes than be surprised at the election?"

She kisses me and rests her head against my shoulder as I gently sip from the bottle, looking in the distance. It might be the alcohol or Sophie's words, but my chest feels less heavy and warmer. What if Burlington unknowingly presented us with an opportunity? A chance to remove the weeds from our garden? One we never considered ourselves, offering unconditional trust to people from the get-go.

We stare at the commune for a little longer when we spot Mango making his way up the hill, his paws leaving no marks on the grass. He curls up at our feet. I also see Gerrard and Patience coming up, bringing a bottle of wine.

"Sounds like you two were having a party without us," says Patience with a big smile on her face. "I say we drink this now, leave no wine for our guests tomorrow."

"I think they drink cider," I say jokingly.

She smiles and gives Gerrard a little nudge as he keeps his gaze down like a guilty child caught in trouble.

"I'm sorry, mate. Shouldn't have gone about and told people."

I extend my hand to shake his. "I'm sorry for not addressing it myself earlier."

"Good, now kiss," says Sophie, causing Patience to chuckle. I blow an air kiss to Gerrard as Sophie sighs, disappointed.

We all sit down and enjoy a chilled Riesling from the early 2010s. The sun begins o set, but the moment feels so calm and soothing.

"Patience, did you see Gerrard coming home last night?" I ask.

"No—I was dead asleep? What happened?"

I burst out laughing.

"You should've seen him. Your man looked like prime Rambo with stripes on his face, hiding in the bushes."

"My Ron Weasley warrior," she says, laughing and rubbing his back.

"Well… at least I was camouflaged and observing from afar instead of being captured by them."

"You jokester," I add. "They saw you. They even had their rifles pointed at you." A sudden pause halts the laughter, and the atmosphere shifts. Patience is staring at me, ready to burst.

"What do you mean? Were they threatening Gerrard?"

"No," I say as I lay my glass down, realising what I said might have worried her. "Chris had a gun pointed at Burlington, and he said to lay it down as they have guns pointed at the nerd, too. I never saw them but didn't want to risk anything."

Patience takes a sip of wine and stares into the distance, almost as if calculating her next move. She appears calm, but I can tell a fire has been stoked in her.

"Well…" she adds, "At least we know they have options beyond talking, I guess. I think having some rifles on standby in case tomorrow goes wrong would be wise."

I do not want to agree, but Patience's suggestion sounds sensible. After all, we do not know these people and what they are capable of. The tension seems to have reached her too far beyond all the calm words she shared with others.

"Fine. Within reach but not within view. Should their intentions be pure, I want us to be hospitable and nothing else." I conclude, making sure that we're all in agreement.

"What about Chris?" asks Sophie. I look at Patience and Gerrard, but neither of them want to say anything.

"I say we don't mention this to him yet. He seems a bit on edge already, and I'd rather not set a fuse off unnecessarily. He has his pistol by his pillow and knows where it is if he needs it."

They agree, and with the bottle finished, we make our way to the mess hall. This time, it wasn't my turn to cook. Charlotte took over the kitchen and prepared some duck breast with mash and gravy. I'm so proud of her—she's really stepped up and learned a lot. I don't know if it's the food or the breakfast speeches, but the atmosphere is more relaxed. I see people drinking some wine and laughing sporadically across the hall. I look at Gerrard, who has a wide grin on his face.

"I brought up the good wine," he says, smiling. "I knew this would diffuse the tension."

He winks at me and carries on eating. I see Charlotte at one of the tables, trying to seek my approval. I raise my glass and nod at her proudly. She's all smiles.

Shouts of children outside my tent wake me up. I turn to see Sophie sleeping soundly with Mango by her side. I get up and step outside to take in some fresh air. The sky is overcast, and some menacing clouds seem to be coming from the west. I wave to Byron, who's heading to the kitchen. He nods, then buries his head and keeps walking. I see people standing outside their homes. The air is filled with expectation.

I head to the kitchen to ensure lunch preparations are going well.

"Morning, Chef," greets Charlotte as the other volunteers turn around.

"Morning, guys. All good?"

"Yes, all good," she responds. We are exercising great restraint in not dropping any rat poison in the soup."

I smile. "Keep it close; we may need it for dessert," I say.

The streets are buzzing with people. Never before have I seen it so lively. Sounds of heavy footsteps can be heard near the main gates. A small, jester-looking man is holding a megaphone.

"Ladies and gentlemen of the Hounslow commune. Please welcome his excellency, Sir Burlington!"

Everyone stares at the gate as the short man starts singing into the megaphone, what I assume to be the hymn of the Black Pyramids:

"Hail, hail to the rising light,
Where the peaks are clear and the future's bright,
Order guides us through the night,
For the Pyramid, we stand and fight!"

The rhythm is reminiscent of early 2000s Brit-pop. In fact, I think they might have plagiarised a famous Oasis song. Nevertheless, Burlington is wearing a long coat, with a British flag pinned on the left side of his chest and a Black Pyramid pin on the right.

"Are those his nipples?" Sophie whispers to me as I struggle to contain my laughter.

He wears a baton and smokes a pipe, giving strong Churchill vibes. Behind him are two men carrying baskets and a few more with rifles on their backs. I make my way to the front, next to Patience and Chris.

"Good afternoon!" he greets us whilst making a sign to the men behind him. "For our guests, please."

They offer Patience several baskets with European goods, leaving them at her feet. I spot some jars of olives, some French wine and cheese. One of them comes towards me with a carrier that he opens to reveal a shiny silver chef's knife.

"Huh," Burlington smirks. "You don't think we would've forgotten about the famous Chef, do you?"

From the crowd, Gerrard steps forward.

"What about the guns, fash?" he asks ironically. Burlington turns around as if taken by surprise by his guards.

"Aw, them? Protection. We have a, how to put it, unfair reputation. You never know who might misjudge us before they hear us."

Patience looks at me, a bit worried. I'm a little distracted by the shiny knife. I feel like my emotions have been bribed. Damn, this guy got to me. Japanese steel, too.

"Oh well, let's hear ya then," adds Gerrard as he makes his way to the mess hall. "Hurry up, we don't have all day," he says, ushering people inside. He is still pissed off, and he doesn't do a great job at hiding it, either.

Inside the hall, we all enjoy the food that Charlotte and the volunteers have made. Burlington eyes me up.

"You made this, Dominic?"

I swallow the broth before answering.

"No–ahem," I say as I choke slightly. "It is my recipe from the book, but it's Chef Charlotte's execution."

"Ah," he replies, "Yes, the famous Chicken Soup you made in the early days of the apocalypse. I did ask one of my chefs to try making it once, but it wasn't nearly as good."

I smile and accept the compliment on behalf of Charlotte. Patience rises and draws the attention of the hall towards her. There is an awkward silence.

"Folks, we have guests today, no doubt you have noticed by their grand entrance. They are here to address us and share their vision for London."

She pauses and sighs for a second.

"No doubt you have all heard that the Council meets on Monday, and there is a strong indication that we will have city-wide elections as the army plans on stepping back. With that in mind, I invite Mr Burlington to—"

"Sir!" interjects the jesterish fellow.

Patience gives him a death stare from above.

"Commune, I give you Sir Burlington."

Some scattered applause can be heard, and all eyes are fixated on Burlington, who has a presence about him.

He cleans his mouth with a napkin and stands at the head of the hall, his posture relaxed, his expression calm and composed. A couple of his goons flank him, their eyes searching the room with a quiet intensity.

Burlington begins to speak, his voice smooth and

confident, carrying easily over the hushed room.

"Ladies and gentlemen of the Hounslow Commune," he begins with a warm tone, almost conversational. "I must say, it is an absolute pleasure to stand before you today. I know so much about your remarkable community—how you've banded together in these difficult times, how you've shown resilience, compassion, and a dedication to one another that is truly inspiring to a city that has forgotten what a community is."

He pauses, letting his words settle, allowing a few of the more receptive members of the commune to nod slightly in agreement. I realise there's a skill to this—Burlington knows exactly how to draw people in and make them feel seen and valued.

"You've built something incredible here," he continues, eyes sweeping across the room. "A place where people can find shelter, safety, and a sense of belonging. In a world turned upside down, you've created order out of chaos, a sanctuary in a storm and a place where each contribution is valued. That is what we value as Black Pyramids—contribution."

I glance around the room. Some of the tension seems to be easing as if Burlington's praise is slowly disarming the more sceptical among us. But there's something in his voice, an underlying current that makes me wary, that keeps me on edge. I see Gerrard slightly twitching in his seat, with his leg stomping aggressively.

"But as we all know," Burlington says, his tone shifting ever so slightly, becoming more serious, "Rebuilding is no easy task. It requires more than just good intentions—it requires strength, unity, and, above all, leadership. The kind of leadership that can guide us through the dark days ahead, that can help us rebuild not just a community, but a society." He scans the room, making sure his words land.

There it is, the subtle shift. His words are still carefully chosen and polished, but the underlying message is clear. He's no longer just praising us—he's laying the groundwork for something more, something that feels like it's inching closer to a rhetoric we've heard before.

"In times of uncertainty," Burlington continues, "it's easy to lose our way. It's easy for divisions to arise, for fear to take hold. But we must resist that. We must stand together, unite in our purpose, and recognise the need for a strong hand to guide us. A society that values those who bring value and tries to help those who do not integrate into a system that works for the benefit of all."

Chris stiffens beside me, his eyes narrowing as Burlington's words hang in the air. He knows what's coming, and so do I. Burlington is no longer just talking about leadership—he's talking about control, power, and the worthy and unworthy. But he's doing it in an almost imperceptible way, threading his true intentions through a veil of concern and reason. *Sympathy!* That's what MBGA never showed. He acknowledges those who need help, but only to get them to a level *deemed useful to society*.

"Now, I'm not here to dictate how you should live your lives," Burlington says, raising his hands in humility with his head bent. "Far from it. You've built something here that is admirable, something that should be preserved and protected. But I am here to offer a vision of a London that rises from the ashes, stronger and more united than ever before. A London that works." It's an impeccable Hollywood performance so far; I'm equally terrified and mesmerised.

A few members of the commune nod, clearly taken in by his rhetoric. Burlington's words are compelling, persuasive, and delivered with a confidence that makes it hard to argue with him. I see Mrs Patel leaving the room, shaking her head.

"We need a strong foundation, built on trust, order, and the understanding that sometimes, difficult decisions must be made for the greater good."

I can feel the room beginning to sway, his words planting seeds of doubt and questioning whether our way of life—our focus on collective decision-making and openness—is enough to face the challenges ahead.

"And that's where we come in," Burlington continues, his voice steady, reassuring. "The Black Pyramids are not here to impose but to lead. To help guide, to help strengthen. To work with you, to ensure that what you've built here doesn't just survive, but thrives. Together, we can create something truly great that will stand the test of time and ensure a future for all of us."

He ends his speech with a warm and inviting smile, but a coldness in his eyes sends a shiver down my spine. The room is silent momentarily, the weight of his words hanging heavy in the air. Then, slowly, a few members of the commune begin to clap, hesitant at first but growing in confidence as others join in.

I remain seated, my hands still, my thoughts racing. Burlington's speech was everything I feared it would be—subtle, persuasive, and deeply, deeply dangerous. As the applause dies down, Burlington steps back, his smile widening as he sees the effect his words have had. Gerrard and a few others leave the room before some bottles of wine are brought to the tables by Burlington's men.

I can't shake the feeling that we've just opened a door that should have remained closed. Patience catches my eye from across the room, and I can see the concern etched on her face. She knows, just as I do, that this is far from over.

With the luncheon ending, we escort our guests to the main gates. A few people step from the crowd to extend a handshake to Burlington. He adores it, as if he were trained at Eton College, a ready-made political leader. As he's about to step out, he turns towards me.

"Thank you. I hope to keep in touch soon as the election gets organised," he says, thanking me while avoiding Patience's extended hand and opting for a nod instead.

Gerrard comes out of nowhere, rushing from the crowd, emptying a milk bottle all over Burlington.

"Take this fascist." He grabs one of the gift baskets and throws it at him. "Take all your fascist bribes with you, too. Find some other bootlickers."

The jester's jaw drops to the ground, watching the scene unfold, and can't help but squeak in a high pitch into the megaphone. He draws a tiny dagger from his hip and points it at Gerrard from a few safe feet away.

Burlington's guardsmen snap to attention, raising their rifles at the front row of Hounsies.

Without hesitation, Patience and a few others reach behind haystacks, pulling out their weapons. Within a matter of seconds, I find myself in the middle of a stand-off, frozen, with guns surrounding me. Chris is watching the scene surprised, shouting, "Calm down," and getting in front of the Hounsies, urging them to lay down their weapons.

Burlington steps in front of his men, hand raised, with milk dripping from his hair, which I now realise is a toupee as he tries to rearrange it. His arm lowers, making his guards stand down.

"Now, now", he adds, using a handkerchief to clean his face. "Nothing wrong with some healthy opposition. No harm done, but I'd advise you, Dom, to make sure this does not escalate—we've had enough political violence over the past year, surely?"

A bit frozen from the guns drawn, I remain speechless and nod silently in agreement as Burlington instructs his men to leave. The Jester returns briefly to grab the Camembert from the milk-sodden gift basket.

"What?" he looks at me, sensing my judgment. "Good cheese is hard to come by." He picks it up and starts running comically to catch up with the group. Mango is standing on one pole by the gate, making sure to hiss at each Black Pyramid member walking past. When the Jester reaches out to pet him, he meows and slaps the Jester with his paw over the back of his neck.

"Meow Bitch, Fuck off."

With the Black Pyramids gone, people are starting to retreat to their homes, and all I hear are whispers. Opinions are divided, with some feeling that what Burlington said made sense. The commune is not without its challenges. No one set out to achieve utopia here; understandably, some members have found it difficult to adapt.

"Are we going to talk about this?" asks Patience, seeing me ready to leave.

"Tomorrow, I think we should all sleep on it and see how we feel tomorrow." She sighs. "Fine—going to catch up with Gerrard. Make sure the nerd doesn't chase them or something."

I hug her. "Tomorrow!" I take Sophie's hand from the crowd and depart for our tent. Today we eat dinner at home, leftovers. Walking past Edna's shop, I can't help but notice Mrs Patel sitting on the stairs rubbing a photo in her hands. She spots me, and before I get to say something, she interjects.

"I'm okay, Dom; don't worry," she says as she gets up and passes me the photo. "Don't forget, though, that it didn't all start with violence. It started with sweet talk and the need for order. I'll see you tomorrow," she says as she rubs my shoulder and leaves. I look at the photo of her and Mr Patel in front of the shop when they opened it. I miss the Bossman.

The rain finally starts to pour after threatening us all day, washing and cleansing the ground soiled by the Black Pyramids' presence.

SLICING THE BREAD

"Catch, Mango!" I say as I tease him with a cable I found. He jumps around trying to catch it, but I pull it away at the right time.

"Meow bitch—give me it."

He jumps and twirls in the air, but to no avail. I decide to let him win one so on one jump, I decide not to pull. He grunts as he drags the cable out of my hand and takes it behind the tent, where Bowie is watching him attentively.

Sophie was watching the whole ordeal, cheering for Mango.

"Did he eventually win?" she says with a smile.

"Fair and square," I admit.

"Breakfast at Patience's this morning?" she asks.

"Yeah, let me grab some bread from the kitchen."

It's the day of the dreaded Council meeting, and Patience suggested we gather for breakfast. As we approach their place, the smell of freshly ground coffee sends shivers down my spine; I feel that she left the kitchen window open on purpose. We knock, and she greets us with a warm smile, leaning towards us to whisper.

"Mrs Patel is here too. She stayed over last night."

We walk in and greet Mrs Patel, who is reading a book. She lifts her eyes and lights up when she sees us.

"Where's Gerrard?" I ask Patience, at which she points to the other room.

"Doing research," she says, using hand gestures for ironic quotes.

"Ah! Fuck off, Vylan Tusk!!!" can be heard from the other room. We decide to check on him. He turns towards us, agitated.

"This prick. He has a pop-up of updates every time you log on now." He turns the screen towards us. "Look—three pages of his fucking thoughts and opinions. You can't skip them! The internet slot is gone by the time you get through them."

"What's he saying?" asks Sophie curiously.

"Just the usual. Bragging about other people's work that he claims is his. Geo-political opinions. Climate change. What isn't? It's like he has a public kink, wants everyone inside his head." Says Gerrard, vividly irritated. "I'm trying to read more about how these Black Pyramids came to life, but every time I search for something, I get to a dead end."

"Come get some coffee," suggests Patience. "The Pyramids will be there later, and the coffee will get cold."

We return to the main room, where the smell of coffee is replaced by what could only be described as Triple Mango. I see Chris sitting beside Mrs Patel, showing her how he can blow smoke circles with his vape.

"Stop that bullshit," says Patience. "We don't need that smell in here."

We sit and have a moment of silence, just enjoying that fresh coffee. It tastes so different; the flavour hits all the right spots.

"It's from the gift bag. Brazilian coffee," says Patience, to which Gerrard spits it out.

"Aw, stop being a child; I'm not a Black Pyramid because I drink their coffee", she rebuts.

"Speaking of which…" I feel the need to address the elephant in the room. "Thoughts?"

Everyone looks down, trying to get their words right, whereas Gerrard bursts without hesitation.

"Fascists. Every one of them. I don't buy this new-age bullshit. This is MBGA all over again."

He stops as if he expects any of us to counter his point. We don't. I think we all feel a whiff of the same old fascist smell.

"So," he continues, "I say no more visits, no more gift bags, fuck them and what they represent."

"They'll go for elections, though. It doesn't really matter what we want; it's about the whole city. What do you suggest we do if they win? Take the commune off the ground and place it outside the M25?"

"We fight them." He instantly responds.

"You're not serious, are you?" responds Chris. "They seem more organised and much larger than what they let us see when they visited us. Do you really believe that the whole organisation is seven blokes and a jester?" Silence takes over the room.

"Maybe we do fight them," Sophie interjects uncharacteristically. Not one for fighting, she should be the last to suggest this.

"Babe?" I ask confused.

"No, not with guns. The election."

We all think about it for a second.

"But—our principles for the commune are far from centralised government. We never set out to oversee London, just our patch here," I add.

"It will be gone," says Mrs Patel. "The commune will be gone if they get into power. If we fight them in the election, we're not fighting just for London but for the existence of this place."

"I agree," says Patience. "We need to win that Mayor seat."

"How would we run though?" I ask, "And who would run?"

They all look down, not wanting to suggest a name. Chris draws from the vape.

"You, lad," he says, fixing me with his eyes. "Who else is a celebrity in this city? Who brought people together through food in times of despair?"

I shake my head and try to fight back.

"But I don't want this. I'm not a politician." I keep

shaking my head. "No, no."

Mrs Patel gets off her seat and joins me on the couch to my right. She places her hand on my knee.

"You can do it as you've done it before. It's a different type of fight but for the same principles."

I look at her, and her eyes are begging me. Chris seems relaxed, Sophie's hand on my back tells me she's in. Patience pours another cup of coffee, looking hopeful. Gerrard stops twitching, nodding gently as if he is running many scenarios in his head, all turning out favourably.

"Yes!" he bursts. "You have to do it."

The whole room is in agreement, apart from me. Are they seeing something I can't? It's like my mind is shaking, but I look at my hands, and they are still. They're usually quick to tell me when I'm nervous, but not this time. I look around the room, and all I see is family. For over a year, I've sworn to protect them. This time, I may not even need to pick up a rifle. Perhaps it's worth a fight.

I smile and nod.

"Fuck it—let's have it."

The Council chambers are packed in anticipation of

the election, you can tell people have started to organise. The Black Pyramids have shown up in large numbers, and they seem to be wearing a uniform reminiscent of the times of our great-grandparents. The black shirts are all tucked in, and they all have a pyramid belt buckle, keeping their black trousers tight on the hips. The black boots complement the outfit terribly. At any other time, I would've thought they were just some punks from Camden.

As we walk through the room, we come across Fowler.

"Dom! Patience!" he jumps as if he wants to hug us, but cannot because the other army members are around. "How is life in the commune? I'm considering retiring there once we finish with the election."

"Cap, why are you guys doing this?" interjects a rather concerned Patience. "Surely, you're not blind to these Pyramid guys."

He checks his surroundings and makes a sign to follow him to an adjacent room. Making sure no one hears, he speaks low, "They threatened more instability unless we allow the election to take place. The army is weakened from the MBGA times. We are out of practice and proper weapons, and the Europeans do not want to help the peacekeeping efforts. It has become impossible to run this with their numbers growing so steadily."

"But how can they overpower you?" I interrupt, "How do they have access to so many weapons?"

"We…" he pauses and shakes his head, ashamed, "We don't know. Genuinely." Patience puts her hands on her hips and looks disappointed. Fowler checks the room again. "I sent a battalion to some trouble in the Barking market the other week. They had twice our numbers. Twice as weapon-heavy. My guys had to retreat."

"So, you're just going to allow them to take over?" asks Patience.

"They are populists, Patience. They want to win power, not take over. They want people to buy into their cause. I think they can be defeated with ideas rather than weapons."

I sit and ponder for a second on Fowler's words.

I glance at Patience, her eyes burning with frustration, and I can feel the same heat rising in me. *Populists?* Sure, they want power through influence, but that doesn't mean they won't spill blood to get it. I've seen what the Black Pyramids are capable of and what lengths they'll go to if they feel cornered. Fowler's right about one thing—people are buying into their rhetoric. But how long before the Pyramids stop trying to *convince* and start *forcing*?

I can see the cracks in Fowler's confidence. The man who once led us into battle now feels…hesitant and unsure. The army, our supposed safeguard, is weakened. London's chaos has spilt over, and no one wants to touch this mess, let alone clean it up.

"The army will get behind anyone who wins them over." Fowler admits, "But they need to win the popular vote."

I muster the courage to share my thoughts on running with Fowler. Patience nods as if encouraging me to go for it.

"In that case, Cap…"

"Order! Order!" can be heard from the main room. Fowler is standing still, waiting for me to finish my thoughts.

"Let's go," says Patience, "I'm sure things will be clear soon."

The hall has gone eerily silent as General Strobinski, one of the few remaining generals from the old military, steps up to the podium. His uniform is crisp. Behind him, a flag hangs loosely, its colours faded but recognisable—a symbol of a United Kingdom that no longer exists.

He opens the meeting with a moment of silence, asking everyone to bow their heads for those lost in last week's attacks. As the silence stretches on, I can feel the eyes of the room subtly shifting towards the Black Pyramids. We all acknowledge them, we all fear them, and their presence is sucking out all the air in the room. They sit stiffly, their faces carefully neutral, but there's a tension. They know they're being watched.

After a long beat, Strobinski raises his head and clears his throat.

"Citizens of London," his voice is calm but carries the authority of someone who has seen too much war. There's an audible sigh. "We are here today to discuss the future of our city. Our home. For too long, London has been on the edge of chaos. But we've held on, and we've survived. You, all of you, are why we're still standing." His words are met with nods and murmurs of agreement, but there's no joy in the room, just dread and anticipation. Everyone knows why we're here. Everyone knows what is about to happen.

"However," Strobinski continues, his tone hardening, "there are factions in this city that seek to undermine the fragile peace we've built. We cannot allow London to fall into further disarray. And that is why, after much consideration, the Council and the army will be stepping back to allow the people to decide the future of this city." There's a collective intake of breath.

The Black Pyramids start hugging and congratulating each other as if they had won the election before it started. Even though we all knew this was coming, hearing it said aloud makes it real.

"We will have elections," Strobinski says firmly. "Every citizen will have the opportunity to vote for the leader they believe will guide London back to stability. We need someone who can rebuild not just the infrastructure but the trust that has been shattered."

He pauses, his eyes scanning the room. The Black Pyramids sit quietly now, but their expressions emanate excitement. Burlington sits at the edge of his seat, watching like a hawk, waiting for the prey to fall into its lap. I can almost hear his mind working, calculating.

"Let me be clear," Strobinski continues, his voice lowering. "The army will remain neutral. We will support the people's will, no matter what that will is."

Murmurs start to erupt in the room, and you can see advisors quickly moving around the room like merchants, trying to forge alliances and meetings for their leaders.

"The future of London is in your hands," Strobinski finishes. "It's up to you to decide what kind of city you want to rebuild. Choose wisely."

He steps back from the podium, and the room is filled with hushed whispers. The Black Pyramids are already talking amongst themselves, laughing and cheering. Across the room, other factions look anxious, unsure of what comes next. I see the Duke of Primrose Hill shaking hands with Burlington and receiving a Pyramid pin from the group. As he walks out, I stop him.

"You too, Douche?"

"Oh, come on, Dom. You're playing at utopia while the rest of us are trying to build something functional. People want stability, not fantasy." He sneers, flashing the Pyramid pin like a badge of honour. "You *Dommies* will have to join an orderly society soon. No more playing the hippies."

"Dommies?" I say, trying to hold a nervous laugh. Deep down, I was furious, but I didn't want to give him the satisfaction.

"Yes, you fool, it is a play on words with your name and commies, which is what you are."

"Proud of yourself for that one, are you?" adds Patience.

"Whatever, I look forward to seeing you at the bottom of the social order," he says as he walks out singing, *"Hail, hail to the rising light, where the peaks are clear, and the future's bright…"*

Before we leave, I approach Fowler as he gives his orders to some patrolmen.

"Leaving, Dom?"

"Yes—one last thing," I say as I drag him away for a chat. "I will run. Might need your help."

His face is filled with excitement, and for a sombre army man, he is terrible at hiding his giddiness.

"Really? Amazing—what can I do?" his eyes are wide open, awaiting instructions.

"We might need some logistical help from the army. Do you think you can influence Strobinski and others?"

He looks around the room.

"Yeah—I think I can do that." He nods, shaking my hand. Rest assured, the army will be by your side—not overtly, but send your requests through me, and I'll make sure they reach the right ears."

I smile and grab one SPAM roll from a waiter on my way out. From the corner of my eye, I see Burlington discussing with a couple of leaders from the east settlements. I can't help but overhear him whispering, *"And you'll make sure of that?"* to one of them. He notices me, smiles and nods, almost dominant. As if I'm completely blind to the fucking he's about to dish out—to me and all of London.

Back at the commune, Sophie and Gerrard are waiting by the gates. Gerrard is visibly excited, like a Golden Retriever pacing around, his invisible tail wagging.

"Come," he says.

He takes us back to his place, and one of the rooms is packed with Post-it notes and a makeshift whiteboard filled with writing that I can't decipher yet. Gerrard stands in the middle of the room, his arms spread open in a *"ta-da"* fashion. I'm a bit stunned and do not understand what's going on. Sophie grabs my hand, "Welcome to your campaign headquarters."

FOOD FOR THOUGHT

Walking through the commune, a hundred versions of myself stare back at me. Posters are everywhere, slapped onto walls, stalls, and even some tent doors. The photographer told me to look "friendly but determined". In the image, I'm holding a plate, a map of London resting on it, held together by a multitude of diverse hands. Above my head, bold letters spell out: **Dom. A mayor for all of London. Food for Thought.** The symbolism is obvious—London should work for all, not be divided by social order.

"You've got this, right? It's just like cooking... but with, you know, politics," I tell myself as I stand in the middle of the commune's main square, watching half the village try—and mostly fail—to hang up campaign posters featuring my face. Patience scolds Byron for using too much tape, and Gerrard is arguing with Sophie over the font size on the flyers. Meanwhile, Mrs. Patel is chasing Mango away, who's decided that the stack of leaflets is his new

scratching post. It's chaotic, messy, and so far removed from anything resembling a proper political campaign that I can't help but laugh. *Mayor Dom.* Now, that's a recipe for disaster. Having won the font argument, Gerrard joins me and watches the commune's efforts by my side. He wraps his arm around my shoulder.

"Who would've thought it?" he says, staring proudly as Abu lifts one flag made from an apron.

"This look right to you?" Abu asks, holding the apron at full mast.

"Leave it at half-mast, please. Something inside me is dying." I say as I cringe a bit at this new reality. Gerrard laughs.

I see some people by the shop rolling their eyes at the sight of the flag. I get it. I don't feel too comfortable about it either.

"Come," Gerrard instructs, "Got something to show you."

He takes me back to the campaign HQ, where the room is packed. Sophie intercepts us at the door and shows me some hand-drawn posters with ridiculous food puns. I scrutinise them.

Cooking up a better future. "Really?"

She smiles, and her eyes are glowing. You can tell she loves being involved.

"Ah, I love this one," says Gerrard as he picks up another. ***Seasoning London with Hope***.

I cringe even more.

"Dom!" I hear Patience shouting from the other room. I follow the noise.

I walk in to see Patience with Gomes, the famous Brazilian Chef from Camden. Before the conflict, Gomes was a regular guest on Gordon Ramsay's shows and he owned a chain of restaurants around the North West. I am starstruck and in pure self-awkwardness, I do a half-bow and greet him.

"He's got a proposal for you, Dom."

"Yes," he says with a brief pause. His clothes are a bit scruffy, and his beard has a few loose hairs. He hands me a promotional flyer for London's next big event, another one of the Council's attempts to bring the city together. "I want to invite you to be a competitor at Cookfest. Thousands of people will be attending from all over London, just a week before the election. It could be a great platform for you to speak to people!"

I am humbled by Chef Gomes's invitation. I try to

avoid making too much eye contact, still starstruck, passing him the flyer back.

"Chef, I've got no skill to match you or the others."

"Shut up," he interrupts me with the well-known straightforwardness of Brazilian people. "We need you to fight these motherfuckers. The event will be live-streamed. Think about how many people you can reach."

Vylan Tusk has extended internet slots for the election. In his newsletter/update/thought diarrhoea, he claimed himself a lover of free speech. He wants this election to be run "fairly" and wants people to have access to information.

"To help fuel the campaign," Gomes says as he moves sideways to reveal a box packed with steamy plastic containers.

"Is that...?" I ask with a half-watering mouth. My eyes widen, and my nostrils inhale the aromas.

"Feijoada, yes," he says, completing my sentence. My heart warms. If being a politician means receiving gifts of support like these, then why stop at London? I joke, of course; If I were a bribeable person, food would be the way to do it. *I do not care for gold, just deep-fried cod.*

I shake his hand and thank him as he departs to his

settlement, which without a doubt will be expecting his return. Like us, Camden is a free-for-all kind of society. They don't have a leader, just a board of former punks who ensure some order in the chaos. I've heard tell of the plethora of debauchery, heavy drug taking and great rock and roll which is nothing new for that area.

Gerrard pops in with his laptop and shows me a website he created for my campaign.

"LonDom.com?" I say, questioning his choice.

"Yeah, but look," he says as he clicks on **Enter Website.** An animated chef walks in from the side and opens a menu. It zooms in, and it says *Manifesto*. It's empty.

"What do you think?" he says excitedly, seeking my approval.

"Looks like empty promises to me," I replied jokingly.

He looks at the empty manifesto. "Aw yeah, but the animation is cool, yeah?"

It was pretty cool.

.....

I'm back in the kitchen, but it's not my usual kitchen. The stove is a massive stone structure, like something from an ancient temple. The walls aren't brick, they're made of cookbook pages, fluttering gently like they're alive. Each time I reach out to grab one, it crumbles in my hands and slips away.

The counters are covered with piles of vegetables—potatoes with human faces, all whispering at once. "Don't peel me," one says, "You'll never manage!" another laughs. I pick up a knife, but it's made of paper, flimsy and useless. I try to chop, but the vegetables keep sliding away, wriggling off the cutting board like slippery fish. They're mocking me, spinning around and morphing into the faces of Burlington, Fowler, and Gerrard, each of them grinning in turn.

Above me, the ceiling cracks open and rains down campaign flyers, each one featuring my face. A massive chef's hat emerges behind the stove, but it's not empty. Burlington's inside, perched like a king. He's sitting at a long banquet table, feasting on the city, his fork digging into pieces of London that are served on silver platters. "London needs seasoning!" he bellows, his voice echoing unnaturally, shaking the walls. "And it's up to you, Chef Dom. Can you handle the heat?"

The ground opens beneath me, and I'm falling. I land in the middle of a massive cook-off, but the judges are wearing robes, not aprons. They have gavels instead of forks and shout, "Vote! Vote! Vote!" The crowd around me starts chanting too, banging pots and pans, but the sound twists into something sinister. Their faces blur into black pyramids, marching, multiplying, surrounding me.

I'm handed a plate of raw, unseasoned beef. The crowd stares at me expectantly, their voices rising. I look for spices and ingredients, but my hands are empty. I try to speak, to explain, but the words die out before they can escape my mouth.

As the pressure becomes unbearable, Sophie appears beside me, holding a whisk like a sword. "Take it, and give these people hope." I start whisking away.

·····

"What the fuck!" I wake up, drawing a big breath in. Mango is curled up on my belly, and I'm back in my tent. I hear commotion outside, so I carefully place Mango on the bed, which, despite my best efforts, is received with a hiss. I step outside, heading towards the racket.

By the main gate, I see the Jester singing his song again. Burlington appears from a much larger crowd of supporters. Some of them bear arms. He stops in the middle of the square, and the villagers halt their activities to watch the scene unfold. He inspects the flag and some banners and smiles as he spots me. I make my way there, and I can see Gerrard being held back by Chris ever so slightly.

"Dominic, what a surprise!" he says with a fake grin.

"I could say the same," I say, extending a hand.

"Yes, we were just about to go canvassing in Ealing and saw the flag from the main road." He looks around the square. "I see campaigning going on here. Are you…" He pauses for a second to look around once more, "…running against me?"

He smiles, but it's not his usual smug, confident smile. Still unused to the idea, I respond with a relatively shallow "Yes." Patience joins me and echoes a much louder "Yes, he is."

He paces around the flag, making us all follow him with our eyes.

"Folks, some will cook, while others will lead." Says Burlington, addressing the commune. "You want a chef to run London? What's next, a bartender for Defence Minister?" A few people laugh, and normally, I'd laugh with them if I weren't the butt of the joke. "Aren't you tired of improvised leadership?" he says, staring at Edna. "Of chaos, of amateurism?" She lowers her gaze, refusing to acknowledge his words, but doesn't deny them.

He turns towards me and spots my clenched fist. I only notice it when his smirk deepens, and I force my fingers to relax.

In a condescending tone, he says, "I like you, Dom. I do. But you're not made for this task. Heck, look at this," he says as he lifts a poster from the batch beside him. "This is childish, Dom." He lets the poster fall dramatically to the ground before extending his arms towards the canvassers. He snaps his fingers, and they start chanting together.

"London needs the Pyramids. A bright future awaits. Vote Burlington."

The chanting is loud, and I'm sure Ealing has heard it already. It's got the aggression of football hooligans but the eerie coordination of Christmas carolers. Released by Chris, Gerrard starts shouting himself, trying to start our own chant.

"London doesn't need ... more fascist shit!" He looks around, but none of the Hounsies join in. His lone voice pales in comparison to the group Burlington brought. He makes a step back beside Chris, who puts his arm around him in consolation.

"See, this is order. Organisation. Common goals," Burlington whispers to me before addressing the commune, again, "Join us at the Grand Rally in Hyde Park this Saturday. The great march for freedom. Hear about what the Black Pyramids can do for you."

I see some people whispering and pondering the invite. Burlington salutes me militarily before returning to his group, who starts moving and singing as they go along.

"London needs the Pyramids. A bright future awaits. Vote Burlington."

As the chanting echoes and fades away in the distance, I see a square shaken by what they just saw. The wind stops blowing in the apron, which now looks like a rag. Is it all pointless? Do we even have a chance if all it takes is a chant to shake my people? I know he just tried to intimidate me; I'm aware, I'm just surprised at how effective it was.

"Listen here," shouts Patience, sensing the silence and stunned crowd. "I'm not going to tell you who to vote for," she stares at Edna, "Or who to support. I will remind you, though, that this commune, the success of it, wouldn't have happened if it wasn't for this guy." I can see some Hounsies nodding, following Patience as she moves around, staring them down.

"Remember the revolution. Remember the radio message you heard in Richmond, Acton, and Ealing. You want order? We've had *order* before. It ended with bombs in the Thames and bodies in the streets." She paces slowly but sternly around a circle that has formed around the flagpole. She looks Hounsies in their eyes as if she's speaking to each of them individually.

"Dominic may not be a politician, but I'll take an honest man over a 'leader' who talks in platitudes any day. Actions, not words." She lifts a flyer in the air, reading the slogan out loud. **"The proof is in the pudding."**

I burst out laughing, and everyone follows. The atmosphere quickly relaxes, and I pick up the poster that Burlington dropped.

Slicing Through the Nonsense, Serving Real Solutions! it says. I lift it and show it around.

"Shall we get back to slicing through nonsense?" I say to a cheering and energised crowd. The wind wooshes again through the apron, which now proudly towers over the square.

Later that night, I need to sway some voters by cooking a delicious meal for the commune. The temperature drops a bit over the evening and given the abundance of potatoes we recently secured from the market, I think a stew could warm people's hearts. I'm slicing potatoes with Sophie, and we exchange looks and hopeful smiles. Both of us feel the storm brewing ahead of us, but neither of us wants to give way to doubt.

"I had a weird dream earlier," I tell her. "You handed me a whisk and told me to give people hope."

She laughs. "You sure it wasn't whisky?"

"Thank you," I say, stopping my slicing. "Your love and support have meant the world over the past few weeks. Thank you for believing in me and pushing me further."

She smiles and kisses me on the cheek.

"Thank you for believing in this." She says, gesturing in circles in the air.

Byron pops into the kitchen.

"Chef, the people are in the mess hall and they're hungry."

I look at Sophie and smirk.

"Send the first batch in, Chef", I instruct as Byron confirms and takes the first few Dutch ovens to the mess hall.

As I finish my last batch, I walk into the mess hall as people started leaving. All the extra activity around the campaign has tired people, and as they walk out, they thank me and put their hands on my shoulder. Apparently, the stew was really good. In a now deserted mess hall, one table is left with people. It's Chris, Patience, Gerrard and Mrs Patel. They have finished eating and are having wine for dessert. Sophie and I sit down next to them, and we start to dig into the stew. The flavours combine superbly, and the warmth of the gravy fills me with hope. The potatoes are crisped on the skin, offering that perfect crunch. The beef is *melt-in-your-mouth* tender. Mrs Patel watches me proudly as I eat without a breath.

Byron pops his head in from the kitchen. "Chef, is there anything else needed apart from cleaning?" he asks.

"Have you eaten, Chef?"

"No," he replies. "I'll eat when I'm done, thank you."

I get up, grab a chair from the table next to us, and

pour another glass of wine.

"Come eat. We'll deal with dishes later."

His face brightens. He takes his apron off and joins us. Gerrard takes a big sip of wine and breaks the silence.

"So, this Grand Rally they are talking about. I will be there…"

"The Black Pyramids rally?"

Shocked by Gerrard's words, Patience spits out her wine, and I can see Chris smiling proudly.

STIRRING THE POT

"What about a soufflé?" I ask as I continue making notes and erasing them as I go along.

"Mhm," she mutters, not seeming to hear me.

"I could try a chocolate tart, but I've always sucked at making pastries."

"You could, yeah."

"No. I'll stick to the basics. A simple English trifle. That'll do." I say proudly. Getting no response or reaction from Sophie, I get up from the bed to check on her.

"What's up?" I say as I see her hyper-focused on the laptop.

"Your page." She gasps. "It's blocked or not loading properly."

"What page?"

"The campaign one. It's been taken down."

"Could there be some server issues?" I ask, trying to make sense of it. "What about theirs?"

In contrast, the Black Pyramids page was not only up and running but getting plenty of hits. No wonder—Tusk had made sure to reference it and link it a few times in his daily update.

He had become such a staunch supporter of the Pyramids, it was all he talked about lately. He even prioritised Black Pyramid updates over news from his own company, which had just announced it was training chimpanzees to be fast food workers by implanting chips in their brains. All for productivity. Hail the shareholders of the burger joints and the real estate they own.

This was rotten, though. It seemed that the one self-proclaimed proponent of free speech was now heavily curating our only resource for reaching the masses.

Tusk used to make crass jokes and share opinions no one asked for. Now, he was a mouthpiece for the Black Pyramids.

"What do we do?" I ask, hoping Sophie will have an answer.

There was nothing to be done.

·····

Elsewhere, in the thick of it, Gerrard is already at Hyde Park.

The park is a historic London landmark and one of its large, central gathering spots for people. Gerrard knew he couldn't attend alone, so alongside two commune members, he found a few others attending through various online forums that Dom never cared to ask about. It's just Gerrard's skill to find resources beyond the obvious. Arriving at Lancaster Gate, he joins the rest of the protest, named the Remembrance March in reference to the events of one year ago. He's all smiles, happy to chat with like-minded people, making sure to mention Dom's candidacy to everyone he speaks to.

"The chef?" one asks.

"Yes— it's a purely Anti-Black Pyramid platform. Check the website when you get home. I made the animation."

The shouts are loud and clear, echoing across the main road by the park.

Fuck BP— We will never not be free.

As the protest nears the main event, the scale of the Black Pyramids rally starts to sink in. Black flags line the park's fences, each emblazoned with the ominous pyramid symbol that now feels inescapable. Outside the main gates, three army vehicles are stationed with what can only be described as young lads pretending to be in control. Their eyes look scared. Their soft chins and skinny arms aren't ready to face the energised masses before them. Their captain sits slouched in one of the cars, chewing a deflated hot dog and listening to the radio blaring inside.

"Today, there is a Grand Rally in Hyde Park. Please avoid travelling in the area," DJ Nuke advises his listeners.

Inside the park, the crowd is a sea of black uniforms. Banners wave in perfect unison, the rhythm adding a militaristic undertone to an otherwise festive setting. The air is thick with the smell of beer and street food, but also with something darker—like the quiet dread before a storm. A large stage looms above a crowd that likely numbers in the hundreds of thousands. Sure, not all are fanatics—some might just be curious—but the sheer volume and number of people supporting the Pyramids sends a chill through Gerrard.

In contrast, the protest group barely scrapes together a

thousand people, and only because they were dedicated enough to navigate the algorithmic blockages Tusk has imposed. A metal band blasts from the main stage, giving the atmosphere the feel of a twisted festival. People are drinking, flaunting BP insignias, and some look downright militant. As the protest group edges toward one side of the stage, it becomes clear that some of the more fervent Pyramid fans are growing aggressive. A few scuffles break out—nothing major, yet.

On stage, the jester bounces out, ready to introduce the main speaker. The crowd goes wild, instantly drowning out the protestors.

"London! Are you ready for your future mayor?" he cries.

Burlington steps into triumphal music, on-stage fireworks firing around him. A black pyramid spins from the rafters like a disco ball behind him as he grabs the microphone.

"What about that band, eh folks? True metal for true Londoners," he says, mimicking royal applause with hands that barely touch.

Gerrard tries to boo, but the roar of Pyramid supporters swallows him up. Burlington's speech rolls on—prosperity, order, security, Britishness, order, peace, and more order.

"I look at this mass of people, and all I see are decent folks who want a decent city," he says, pausing for cheers. "Now, some don't want that." He gestures toward the protestors. "They're nothing but terrorists—agents of chaos and anarchy."

The boos intensify. The crowd starts to close in on the protest group.

"In the London of the future," Burlington says, placing a hand to his ear, waiting for the crowd to join in "there's no room for chaos…"

"ONLY ORDER!" The crowd responds in unison.

Gerrard's stomach churns. This isn't just a rally—it's a show of force. His heart races as the shouts grow louder, more hostile. The BP supporters aren't ignoring them anymore—they're ready to strike. Sleeves rolled up, fists clenched, faces twisted with glee at the thought of a fight.

Vans roll up onto the grass. More riot paramilitaries spill out. The appearance of force confirms Gerrard's worst fear. This is a battlefield.

Gas canisters arc through the air. Batons come down indiscriminately. A shout bursts behind him. Shoving.

Jostling. It happens fast. Pyramid supporters surge forward, dragging the 'terrorists' toward Burlington's goons.

Gerrard spins, scanning for an exit. Past a food stall, he spots an opening.

He slips from the grasp of one supporter and dashes through the chaos. A riot officer steps into his path—a boy drowning in his oversized uniform. But his hand doesn't hesitate on the baton.

The blows rain down. Gerrard barely feels the pain. His eyes lock on Burlington, still smug on the stage above it all. For a moment, the world goes still. Burlington meets his gaze and smirks, triumphant and predatory. He waves mockingly, as if to say: *You never stood a chance.*

Gerrard seethes as he's dragged toward the vans. But it's not the bruises that haunt him—it's that smile. He looks around, desperate for help, but none comes.

The junior soldiers outside the gates just watch, powerless. Outnumbered. Outgunned.

"Fuck you, you fascist pig!" Gerrard shouts at Burlington as three men haul him into a van.

·····

I've been out of the loop for hours. When I finally get to Patience's house—our makeshift HQ—Abu has a bloodied nose, and Charlotte is tending to it.

"What happened?" I ask, worried.

Abu looks at me but doesn't respond. From the other room, Chris pops his head around the door with a tilted beret on his head, giving the vibes of a French army commander.

"Get in, we need to talk."

The *war room* was Gerrard's office, and now it is plastered with maps of London and slogans. Inside, Patience awaits.

"Dom, they are actively trying to stop our efforts." She says. "Abu out there is part of the few people who went to other settlements to hand out flyers. They have patrols outside virtually every settlement."

"I think they might've taken down our website too," I add, deflated.

"We need to change tactics," says Chris, "We've been playing defence too much."

I can feel my face getting hotter by the minute. I was not excited about this campaign under normal conditions, but now, with the threat of violence and interference, I feel even sicker to my stomach. However, a sense of duty seems to balance it out. Despite feeling more worried and concerned than before, I also feel more fired up and determined to take this fight head-on. I drag the chair loudly before I sit in it, determined not to show the troops my worries, just my fire. Whatever we do, we must not give in to their intimidation. Not just for us but for the rest of London.

"Okay— I'm open to suggestions," I say to them both as they look at each other, hoping the other would speak first. Sophie walks into the room holding my cookbook.

"This," she says. "This could be it."

"I don't understand," I say, picking up and inspecting the book.

She moves towards the map, giving it a serious look like a proper strategist. Her hands rest on her hips, and she moves her gaze across the map as if looking for a place.

"*Cookfest* is next week, right?"

I nod as Chris and Patience lie back in their chairs, praying for Sophie to pull a magic trick here.

"And you have a notebook filled with new recipes?"

"I do, yes," I respond, equally excited and nervous about her plan.

"We do this," she says as she takes the book from my hand. "You write another one. Say, '*What to eat after the apocalypse*? Pack some recipes, but you also include your manifesto."

"Woah," exhales Chris, jumping from his chair excited and applauding. "I love it."

"I'm not sure I follow," I say, a bit confused.

Sophie gestures towards Chris, passing him the book. She invites him to explain the move to me, whilst she picks a slice of the cake that Charlotte baked this morning.

"Dumbo. There are chefs from all over London there. They all support you anyway."

"Yes, so…?" I say in the same confused manner.

"Tusk is controlling the internet, the Pyramids patrol the streets, but a book…" he says, smiling from ear to ear.

Patience jumps from her chair, too, as understanding dawns, making me the last to catch on.

"A book can be moved around inconspicuously," she says, grabbing the book from Chris. "Gift some books to the chefs there and ask them to share with their settlements."

Sophie drags a chair next to me and grabs my hand. "This isn't just about recipes anymore, Dom. Food brings people together, remember?"

"This can give you a shot to spread your message despite their hurdles. You can't win if no one hears you," adds an excited Chris. I sit down and flick through the pages of my first book.

"What if it doesn't work? How can one book be passed among communities? We're talking millions of people here and three weeks until the election." I look at Patience, seeking some approval. "This is mad, no?"

I stare at the cookbook in her hands. It seems ridiculous initially—how can a bunch of recipes change anything? But then I see the determination in Sophie's eyes, the way Chris nods like we have stumbled onto something big. This isn't about changing everything. This is about getting our message out there, one way or another. If they believe in this plan, I must too. Since there is no alternative, I agree to it, and Sophie pulls out the laptop.

"Now," she says. "Let's start with some soups."

·····

Meanwhile, far from the warmth of any kitchen, Gerrard stares out the narrow window of a van. As it exits the M25 near St Albans, he watches the worried protesters inside trying to reassure each other. A partly destroyed London skyline fades into the distance, swallowed by the countryside's green as it creeps along the main road.

He realises he hasn't left London in almost three years, and the last time he did, it was a bustling city he came back to. One where people of all races and creeds tried to make do—sometimes for better, sometimes for worse—but all under one shared identity: Londoners.

What he leaves behind now is a fractured city where, once again, a strong hand claims it can fix everything with discipline and order. *We never learn* keeps running through his head as he sits silently, not knowing where he's being taken, for how long, or whether he'll ever see Patience or his friends again.

The van brakes abruptly, and a few people topple over. The door swings open, and masked men drag them out one by one. Gerrard spots a massive estate, acres of land stretching out, with no road in sight. As he's taken inside, he sees Black Pyramid flags, maps, and pictures of Burlington pinned to the walls.

"Move on," says one of the men, kneeing Gerrard in the back. He doesn't feel the pain—he's too busy scanning the space as he's moved from the hallway to the stairs, then down to the basement. *Only one van pulled up here,* he thinks, already trying to piece the puzzle together.

The basement, which at first looks like a wine cellar, turns out to be a long corridor of cells hidden behind a false wall.

"Get in," the man barks, shoving Gerrard into one of the cells. Others are thrown into the surrounding ones. Gerrard watches as a teenage girl resists.

"I'm claustrophobic, no, please—" she pleads, but it's no use. A guard slams her face down into a cell.

The men exit and drag the heavy door shut behind them. Darkness settles in. The air is cold, and the only light comes from a tiny window at the far end of the corridor, casting long bars of light across the cells.

"Psst," a voice whispers from across the hallway. Gerrard can barely make out the man's face.

"Are you willing to fight back?" the voice asks.

.....

Cheering. Flags. Light.

I open my eyes and find myself on top of a double-decker bus, moving slowly through a crowd waving Union Jacks. Chris and Patience are beside me, tossing champagne to the joyous public. Everything is bright and unreal, like a parade from someone else's memory. The crowd chants my name—"Dom, Dom, Dom!"—and Sophie stands to my right, smiling and waving as if she were royalty.

"Stop the bus!" I shout, eager to get down and speak to the people, to embrace them. I hurry down the stairs and pause to thank the driver.

It's Mango.

"Are you sure you want to get off?" he asks, his voice calm and heavy with meaning.

"When did you learn how to drive?"

"Are you ready to face your reality?" he replies.

"I am," I say, stepping off the bus with a rush of excitement, ready to greet the crowd.

The moment my foot touches the ground, the world changes. The clouds darken. Rain begins to fall. The crowd transforms into a sea of Black Pyramid supporters, their faces obscured by hoods and torches burning in their hands.

A man steps forward and pulls down his hood. It's Burlington.

"Get him!" he shouts, and the crowd surges forward, surrounding me with a low, eerie murmur.

I try to speak, but the words turn to ash in my mouth. No one hears me. They don't care about truth or justice. They only want order, and I don't belong in it.

I turn to run, but the bus is already vanishing into the darkness.

"Mango, no!" I call out, but it's too late.

Hands seize me. I fight back, swinging my fists, but each time I connect, my targets dissolve into black smoke. The figures close in. I'm dragged into the heart of the crowd, and Burlington's laughter echoes above it all, fading slowly as everything around me turns to black.

·····

"Dom, stop!" shouts Chris as he tries to restrain me. Sophie is on the other side of the tent, and she watches

Chris overpowering and locking my arms in a cross position.

"It was a dream, relax. We have bigger problems."

I shake my head and rub my eyes awake.

"What problems?" I ask, standing up, relaxing and massaging my wrists.

Patience walks into the tent with red eyes as if she had cried all night.

"Gerrard didn't return from the rally."

THE HEAT IS ON

Patience spends the night in our tent as we try to calm her about Gerrard. In the time I've known her, I've never seen her worried like this. Not when bombs were falling on us, not when there were new mouths to feed in the underground. Just now, when Gerrard probably just had a few too many drinks with the protesters. She seems convinced something happened to him at the rally, but this morning's radio confirmed no incidents during the day. Even Tusk's update had plenty of photos of people smiling and enjoying the day out.

A few drinks help Patience fall asleep, and Chris goes out in the middle of the night to look for Gerrard around Hyde Park. There is a lot of noise throughout the night, and hearing the cats and Jamie Foxx hissing and squeaking, we assume it was animals. In the morning, Chris returns without news about Gerrard.

"There was a lot of mess, and some people told me there were fights between counter-protestors."

"Have any of them seen Gerrard?" she asks, her voice filled with worry. Chris shakes his head. "I even showed them the picture," he says, sharing the Polaroid of Gerrard and Patience in front of the sign to the commune. She turns to me.

"We need to go to the river. Speak to Burlington or whoever is there."

Chris agrees, "We need to get some rifles from your house, just in case."

Patience is up in a breath and ready to go. I reluctantly agree.

When we get to Patience's house, a group of people stand in our way, all peeking inside the window. Charlotte leaves the house, rushing towards us.

"They took our stuff," she tells us, trying to catch her breath. Patience runs past her and goes inside.

"What stuff, Charlotte?" I ask her, trying to help her relax. "Breathe, easy."

"Posters, flyers, what they could."

I can hear Edna starting to plant doubts from the back of the group. "Where is Byron?" she says to a couple of men. Patience comes out with tears in her eyes and falls to her knees.

"It's all pointless…". Sophie crouches next to her and wraps her hand around her shoulder. The whole group outside the house is watching them now, and I can hear Mrs Patel behind me shouting, "Stop it!"

"Get out!" can be heard from further back. I notice Edna and a few men trying to get inside Byron's tent. "Get out. Let's check inside your tent."

I grab Chris and we rush there when we see one man dragging Byron out while Edna and the other man get in.

"Hold the fuck up," shouts Chris who stomps through the crowd and grabs the man by the collar. Chris had a level of authority here and was quite an imposing figure. "Let go of him now!" he instructs. Edna comes out empty-handed.

The crowds leave Patience's house and now surround us, awaiting an outcome.

"Was that worth it?" I look at them, disappointed, as if they sought drama and entertainment, moving mindlessly wherever they heard a commotion. I feel the pressure on my shoulders, and I see Chris looking at me and encouraging me to take action.

"You three, on dishwashing duty for the whole week,

clean up the mess you made here. But first, apologies to Byron are in order."

Byron is holding his head down, and his jaw is evidently tensing. Edna gets down and apologises to him while the men help him get up. I turn towards the crowd, trying to defuse the tension.

"Everyone, let's get back to work— we have an election to win in tough circumstances. But we've faced tougher times."

I see some nods of approval, and the crowds disperse. We return to Patience.

"Dom and I will go to the river now," Chris tells her. "Sophie, can you keep Patience company? We'll be back shortly."

Mrs Patel pulls my shirt gently and places a switchblade in my pocket.

"Be careful."

·····

Somewhere outside the M25, in the damp cells beneath a shuttered estate, the sound of banging across the bar wakes the sleep-deprived protesters. The dim light squeezes through the tiny, dusty window at the end of the corridor. As the dull thumping on the stairs above intensifies, Gerrard gets up and locks eyes with Sayid from the cell across. Outside, the noise of car engines starting and indistinguishable chatter permeates the basement walls. The heavy door opens, creaking loudly, and the prisoners start making noise, trying to plead with the guard arriving on food duty, who's throwing digestive biscuits at all the cells. Sayid watches him closely and nods to Gerrard, who grabs his mug and bangs the metal bars.

"What is it you want, ginger?" asks the guard approaching his cell.

With the guard within reach, Gerrard reaches through the bars to push him. The guard stumbles and ends up with his back against Sayid's cell, who grabs him in a chokehold. It lasts for a long, agonising minute, in which all the imprisoned protesters hold their breath while the guard tries to catch his. Gerrard watches the scene with conflicting thoughts as the goon tries to plead. His eyes roll back, and Gerrard signals Sayid to stop.

"Enough! He's out," he shouts when Sayid does not let go. "Stop, he's passed out."

Sayid conforms, and the guard drops to the floor. He picks his pockets through the bars and finds the keys to the cell doors, to the cheers of the rest of the prisoners. Once he frees himself and locks the guard in his place, he proceeds to free Gerrard.

"Thanks mate," says Gerrard. Sayid moves from one cell to another, releasing people. The guard, however, wakes up and starts banging the bars, seeking help. Scared by the possibility of reinforcements, the protesters start running up the stairs. From behind the group, Gerrard spots the protesters outnumbering the remaining guards, equipped just with batons. Punches are landed, some kicks too, and *everybody is kung-fu fighting*, basically. Overpowered, the guards are dragged by the protesters to the cells in the basement. The freed group cheers and hugs each other. They make their way out of the estate, rushing to get back to their homes.

Outside the main door, staring into the vast estate grounds as people run through the field, Gerrard remains frozen.

"You good, mate?" Sayid asks, walking out of the estate, picking up and munching on the biscuits that had been thrown on the floor.

"Not quite," replies Gerrard. "I'm going to stick around a bit. I need to check some things."

"Need help?"

"You've helped more than enough, mate. Pop around Hounslow anytime; we'll serve you a warm meal."

They shake hands, and Sayid starts heading down the dirt road. He is from the South, a long trek from these fields. Gerrard walks back in and through the vast corridors, checking each room. With the remaining guards in their cells and an empty estate to explore, he feels it's time to gather as much intelligence as possible. The main reception room is packed with Black Pyramid campaign materials, pictures of Burlington, and slogans. The arrogance of the slogans makes Gerrard squirm. *Vote Black Pyramids, because why wouldn't you?*

He walks upstairs and finds a locked office that looks like it belongs to someone important. He steps into a room decorated with photos and hunting trophies. On the wall of pictures, there are various important people next to Burlington, but there is one picture that stands out in particular. One of Burlington and Bartholomew Moss shaking hands.

"The bastards, I knew it!" he says to himself. His heart and mind are racing.

On the large wooden desk, there is a copy of *Project Phalanx* stacked on top of a map of London. As he reads through, Gerrard learns more about the true face of the Black Pyramids. The document details a grim vision for the future of London, a plan meticulously designed by the Black Pyramids to reshape the city into a fortress of order and control. The plan focuses on resource reallocation, dividing London's districts based on their economic and political value. The affluent neighbourhoods—Mayfair, Kensington, and Chelsea—are marked in green on the map beneath the folder. These areas will become the central hubs of power, where resources flow freely, reinforcing the dominance of the elites.

In stark contrast, the poorer districts—Croydon, Tower Hamlets, Hounslow—are highlighted in red. These zones are lined up for systematic neglect. The plan involves stripping them of essential resources and turning them into nature reserves, golf courses, and water parks. Plots of land are assigned to property developers, and mock-ups of villas are attached with paper clips. The people in these areas, labelled "non-essential" in the text, would be forced to relocate to the green zones if they prove their worth or usefulness to a society based on an assessment devised by some Black Pyramid scientist. **V.A.L.U.— Verifiable Assessment of Level of Utility.**

Out of curiosity, Gerrard skims through the test, applying his current contributions in the commune. "Damn, I wouldn't even pass," he mutters at the 30% score he gets.

The rest of *Project Phalanx* describes a chilling process of population management. This strategy seeks to classify London's residents based on their productivity and compliance with the Black Pyramids' ideals. Those deemed valuable are rewarded with access to food, water, and medical supplies. Everyone else is gradually marginalised and cut off from these essentials until they either conform or are erased from the city's future. The repeated rhetoric of "re-education" and "reassignment" suggests something far darker than mere relocation—a systematic purging of the unproductive, filtering out diverse thought.

Surveillance and military enforcement will ensure compliance. Propaganda campaigns are already underway, promoting the Black Pyramids' narrative of order and meritocracy. The goal is to manipulate the public into believing this division is necessary for London's survival—that only through harsh control can chaos be defeated.

As Gerrard reads on, it becomes clearer that the

Black Pyramids envision a city where the rich and powerful thrive while the rest are left to rot. Beneath the language of stability and security, it is nothing short of a plan for authoritarian rule—an upgraded MBGA, accounting for previous mistakes.

He can't believe his eyes. He is so engrossed in the plan that he fails to notice a couple of cars pulling into the estate. The slamming of the car doors jolts him back to reality. The main door opens, and he starts looking for possible escape routes. He tucks the document into his waist and walks across the hallway as the voices downstairs grow more alarmed, discovering what has happened. Using the keys they stole earlier from the guard, he opens a door labelled 'Inventory'.

.....

Chris seems concerned as we walk towards the river. Since we spent most of the time walking without talking, I try to address the obvious.

"Worried about Gerrard?" I ask, hoping to pre-empt his thoughts.

"Worried about it all, mate," he says as he takes a drag of his vape.

I wanted to explore his feelings, but like him, I feared

what they might unveil and wondered if it would be counterproductive. Instead, I enact the classic male behaviour of shoving it down as deeply as possible.

"We fight on," Chris concludes, stopping to catch his breath.

"We do," I confirm.

There it is. The old British saying, "What you gonna do about it? *Que sera, sera.*"

At the river, there was nothing. No boat. No sign of life. Just still water. My teeth hurt from clenching my jaw so much. I was ready for anything. Information, fighting, a dead Gerrard. Instead, I was staring at nought.

Where the fuck was Burlington?

.....

Back in the 'Inventory' room, Gerrard tries to make out what is being said in the house from behind the door. He can hear Burlington downstairs shouting at his men. As he turns with his back against the door, his heart beating in his throat, he comes across shelves upon shelves of flyers and posters. He picks one up, and it sounds incredibly familiar: **We don't need international forces holding our national interests back.**

There is a Black Pyramid sticker attached to the upper right-hand corner. Gerrard rips it up only to uncover what he suspected already. He squirms, not out of joy but vindication, for being right all along. He places the sticker back and makes his way towards the window. He looks out and sees the cars driving away fast. To his left, something else catches his eye again. An emergency sign is placed over a large container. Out of curiosity, he opens it. He finds a few masks, pistols and some gas grenades. He checks one of the grenades only to find it has been produced by Burlington & Sons. *Hazardous,* it reads.

Footsteps are sounding up the stairs, and without willing to risk anything, Gerrard stuffs the flyer and the grenade in his pockets and picks up a pistol. The floor creaks behind the door, and he cannot make up whether there's one, two, or twenty goons behind. He holds the pistol tightly and aims at the door. As the door lock twists, Gerrard's pulse hammers in his ears. His hands grip the pistol, fingers trembling on the trigger. Could he do it? The voices outside grow louder. They are close. Too close.

He exhales sharply, shoving the gun into his waistband. Not like this. Not yet. The lock clicks. A second later, he is through the window. The world tilts as he hits the ground, pain jolting up his side. *"Parkour bitches,"* he thinks to himself, rolling on the grass and darting through the fields.

The voices of guards shouting from the window, "STOP HIM!" don't shake him.

Bullets rip through the grass. Gerrard is weaving through the field. The gunfire feels like a deadly rhythm against the pounding of his feet. He doesn't look back. He can't. The ground is ablaze, and his trainers are being tested as never before. "*Usain Bolt, bitches,*" he shouts, alternating his direction every few seconds, avoiding any hits. He reaches the thick woods— the motorway is just a few hundred trees away.

·····

With evening approaching and unable to find anything, we return to the commune.

"Was there nothing in Hyde Park, then?" I ask Chris.

He takes a few seconds before answering, unsure whether to share.

"I didn't tell Patience, but the place looked messy, and I found a bloodied shirt in one of the bushes."

He seems collected, his steps still steady, so I try not to press my fears onto him.

"That could be from anyone, right?"

"Right," he responds instantly.

When we arrived at the commune, another large crowd was outside Patience's home. We walk in to find Patience and Sophie sitting on both sides of a dusty Gerrard, his feet in a bowl of icy water. He spots us and lifts what appears to be a few pages.

"We need to talk," he says gravely.

Whilst Mrs Patel boils some water for tea and Chris escorts people out of the house, I sit on a chair facing Gerrard, who looks concerned. People led by Chris start protesting.

"We need to know the truth."

"We're supposed to be a family," says another. Chris reassures them all and promises that information will be shared. For now, it is easier to discuss in a small group.

"So…" I press Gerrard as Mrs Patel hands him a cup of tea, "Are you okay?"

"Ah, you know me," he says nonchalantly. "Nothing that a bit of paracetamol can't fix."

Patience rubs her hand on his shoulder, clearly happy to have him back, largely unscathed.

"What happened?" asks Chris, getting straight to the point.

He tells us what happened at the rally, the paramilitary, the estate, and the cells. He walks us through what he saw in Burlington's office and what he found in the inventory, showing us the grenade and the flyers. Chris inspects the grenade closely and reads some of the ingredients listed.

"This is the same shit MBGA used a year ago." Same gas, same effects, he tells us.

I'm calculating it all in my head, and it's clear that Burlington is exactly what I feared he was. A merchant of war and, more so, a close friend of Moss and the former regime. I'm furious and get up, pacing the room. Gerrard starts reading from Project Phalanx, and suddenly it all makes sense. It even describes how to influence society to obtain an election. It's like a fascist takeover manual, a step-by-step guide. I look through the window at the commune as people retreat to their accommodations for the evening.

I can't shake the feeling of exhaustion. Of *deja vu*. No matter what we try to achieve and the peace we try to live in, the danger is always around the corner, dressed up as a solution to a problem we never really had. I look around the room. We all lost and saw what happened last time, and we're about to sleepwalk again as a city into the same hands that sought to destroy us.

"So, what do we do now?" asks Mrs Patel. "Surely, we don't return to accepting that it is what it is? That we are powerless?" I feel the photo Mrs Patel shared with me pressing against my chest in my shirt pocket as if it were made from lead. It's like it's actively trying to tell me something, pushing me to do or say something. I pick up the photo and hold it tightly between my palms.

"This is what we do," I say, capturing everyone's attention. "They will use their friendships with Vylan Tusk to sabotage us online and their physical presence to block our in-person efforts. But who's to say we can't play outside their parameters?"

"You mean the cookbook?" Interjects Sophie.

"Yes, and furthermore…Gerrard?"

"Yes, mate?"

"Can you create an unassuming website where we can upload some files?"

His gloomy face suddenly lights up. Over the past year, we've gotten really close. To the point where I don't always need to finish my ideas; he gets them.

"On it!" he says as he reaches for the computer, stepping carefully, his feet still sore.

Confused, Patience watches Gerrard get to work without instructions, "So, what about it?"

"We'll tell Londoners about who they are."

"How can you share that website, though?" Chris asks, "Wouldn't Tusk block it?"

"He would," I say, "But indulge me for a second here. Sophie, how would you feed children vegetables, say, without them knowing?"

She thinks for a second. "I would probably hide it in their food. Mash it, or, I don't know…"

Patience seems to be a bit frustrated with my cryptic tales. "Dom, stop with the technical knowledge; get to the point."

"No," I say as I reach for my first cookbook. "Sophie is spot on." I open the book randomly and extend it to Patience. "You hide it in the food."

BAKING A TYRANT

It's the day of the Grand Rally in Hyde Park. Burlington stands in his private tent, adjusting his cufflinks. The mirror reflects his carefully groomed image—the confident leader, the future of London. Behind him, a younger recruit fidgets nervously.

"You know, sir," the recruit hesitates, arranging his tie. "I read somewhere that you were... different once, before all this."

Burlington smirks. "Different? No. People just never understood me."

The recruit shifts. "Is it true? About your brother? That... that it was personal?"

Burlington grabs him by the collar, staring, his eyes cold. "Everything is personal." He shoves the young recruit aside as he brushes his shoulders. Outside, the crowd is chanting. He straightens his tie and steps out onto the stage, meeting the eyes of thousands as their voices rise.

"Order. Strength. Future."

James Burlington was indeed different. Growing up

in Essex, he had everything a child could want. Expensive toys, private tutors, and a future handed to him on a silver platter. Yet, for all the privilege surrounding him, he was an outcast, standing awkwardly in the background while the world moved around him. His father, the stoic and respected owner of Burlington & Sons, could command a room with a look, but James? He could never quite figure out how to make people like him.

James never quite fitted in. It wasn't just how the other boys laughed, or the foreign words tossed around the playground. It was how effortlessly they belonged, while he stood on the edges, watching.

James had tried, once, to join them. The football game, the easy laughter. But he wasn't fast enough. Not strong enough. The ball slipped from his feet, and a Polish kid took his place without hesitation.

He expected the laughter. He could have lived with it. But what haunted him was something deeper. They never even hesitated. No apology, no second chance, just a quick dismissal, as if he had never belonged in the first place. It wasn't just the game he had lost. It was the unspoken truth behind it. James was disposable. And that, he decided, would never happen again.

"I'm here to remind you that you are not alone. The Black Pyramids will stand with you through thick and thin, today and tomorrow, ensuring you get what you deserve!"

"You deserve prison, fascist!" shouts one protester, her voice quickly drowned out by the crowd jeering at her.

His resentment for the *others* brewed quietly, like a slow boil. He never understood why his privilege never brought happiness. His father, rarely paying attention to young James, never seemed to notice his growing bitterness. "Hard work, James. That's the secret. A poor man does not work hard enough. He spends too much of his free time being jealous," his father would say. James took that lesson to heart, but he twisted it into something darker: the world is split between those who take what they want and those who don't deserve it.

When James turned twenty-three, his father's sudden death left him reeling. James had spent his whole childhood chasing his father's approval, only to find it just out of reach. The man commanded respect without needing to ask for it—power was simply his by right.

James wanted that. Needed it. And when his father was gone, he realised something else: If power wasn't inherited, it had to be taken. He stood by the grave, gripping his younger brother Joseph's shoulder. Their mother, lost in the fog of dementia, didn't even attend. "We'll make him proud," James whispered, though the words felt hollow.

"One year ago," he says, addressing a silent crowd watching his every move, "War was brought upon us. They may have broken our bones, but they couldn't break our spirit!"

The crowd cheers and shouts back, "We fight!"

James smiles. "Their intentions were pure, noble even, but the execution was dreadful. The army is unable to cater to your needs. We don't need settlements; we need a united London!"

With the world in chaos during the pandemic, James took control of Burlington & Sons and shifted its focus. The contracts for military gear expanded beyond boots and vests. He started attending arms conferences—shadowy rooms filled with generals, politicians, and military contractors.

One evening, he met Bartholomew Moss in a dimly lit room filled with cigar smoke and some of the brightest and most decorated military minds. Burlington could still smell the cigar smoke, even now. That night, Moss had leaned in close, his voice smooth as aged whiskey.

"Britain's changing, James. The weak are taking over. You see that, don't you?"

James had nodded. He had always seen it.

"Then let's do something about it," Moss said, puffing hard on the thick cigar.

"They told you that we are all equal," James says, voice steady. "That we all have the same needs or the same ambitions."

The crowd boos. He lets the moment stretch, then smirks.

"I'm here to tell you the truth." He clutches the lectern. "There is a pyramid of needs in all of you."

The phrase lingers in his mind. A pyramid. That's how he'd always seen the world. Joseph had been at the top. Bright, full of potential, studying economics at Cambridge. And what happened? A worthless foreigner had ended him. The far-right media had a field day. MBGA seized the moment, with Moss's voice booming across rallies. "They come here, they take our jobs, and now they take our lives!"

James stood at his brother's funeral, his hand gripping the casket, his heart frozen with grief and rage. The media had called it a "tragic misunderstanding," but James saw it differently. This was proof. Proof that the Britain he loved was under the violent siege of foreigners. That day, his bitterness crystallised into something else. A mission.

He poured his grief into his work. The contracts kept coming, millions flowing in as the government stockpiled weapons. His company developed the infamous "green gas," sold under the guise of peacekeeping but designed for warfare. And while his public face remained stoic, his private dealings with MBGA grew closer. Golfing trips with Moss. Private dinners with military officials. Behind closed doors, they spoke of a Britain reborn, by any means necessary.

"They do not like us for one reason and one reason only." He pauses long enough to build the tension in the crowd. "We believe in Britain. We feel British. And they would rather we hide that."

"No, we won't!" chant the masses.

"At the apex of the Pyramid stands our pride in being British", he says, hands raised in the air, a Union Jack unfurling behind him, fireworks setting off.

"Nothing can be built again without it."

When the bombs dropped, James was caught off guard like everyone else. Sitting in his office with a Congolese Army contract in hand, he watched the news unfold in disbelief. He had thought MBGA was preparing for war, but this... this was something else. And worse, he had been left out. The destruction wasn't just collateral damage but part of a plan he hadn't been privy to.

For the first time, James felt vulnerable and powerless. *They betrayed me*, he thought. Moss had been a liar and a fraud, and James had been loyal to him, until that loyalty was no longer deserved. When the truth about Moss's nature emerged, James didn't hesitate. He fed information to the resistance, not because he agreed with them, but because power belonged to those who earned it. MBGA had betrayed him, and this version of James would not tolerate betrayal.

"When the fighting began, I was there, ready to offer my family's assets to fight back for this city." The crowd applauds frenetically.

"Like you, I am the resistance in this city. And the resistance is far from being done."

It wasn't long before he found a new outlet for his ambitions. Through his friend Vylan Tusk, who controlled the dwindling resources of the internet, James created Phoenix—a dark web forum where like-minded individuals gathered. Here, the seeds of the Black Pyramid were sown, a new organisation with a vision for London's future. A future built on order, control, and class segregation.

The message was too strong to be digested by the masses, and James knew this. Having played with poor kids, he knew that the only way to get their support was to appeal to their pride. *"If only they could feel like they are part of those making order,"* he used to say, *"they will not see order as something to fear."*

Phoenix evolved into Project Phalanx, and the Black Pyramid became its symbol. Burlington recruited former MBGA members, the well-off, and those in positions of power. Though some of his followers wanted direct action, James knew better. Violence alone wouldn't win the people. He needed their loyalty. He needed to be loved.

As violence erupts to the right of the stage, Burlington stands defiant, smirking and clapping ironically. His goons arrive, and they're now handling and arresting the protestors with the crowd's support. The crowd feel like they are bringing order.

"See, folks," he says, pointing towards the protesters. "Chaos. Aren't you tired of it?" He waves to Gerrard as he is dragged to one of the vans.

"The only way forward for this city is through order!"

"Order. Strength. Future." The crowd replies.

COOKFEST

It's the night before *Cookfest*, and I'm still in the kitchen past dinnertime, trying out various recipes that I think can impress. Charlotte is helping me organise my thoughts, taking notes. Luckily, each contestant is allowed a sous chef to assist, so I chose her, given how she's proved herself recently.

"What if we open with a salad?" she says, biting the pen with her teeth.

I'm checking the pantry and doing some mental mathematics about the spices available.

"Or," she says, "we can go with something with more of a kick?" She picks up some dried chillies. "We can make a red Thai soup?"

I'm a bit lost in thought and turn to Charlotte without a response. She places the notebook on the counter and rests against it.

"What's on your mind? Is it the contest or the election?"

I shrug my shoulders. It was both. I had this nagging feeling that all this stress would be for nothing.

"I'm just tired," I say, picking up an apple and throwing it in the air before catching it. "Whatever we do, they have a way to sabotage it, to keep me back. And this… contest," I say as I set the apple down, "What's the point? There are better chefs, it will be live-streamed, and it could be the type of public humiliation I do not need before this election, which could be another setback."

While I'm self-pitying and Charlotte does her best to indulge me, I see Mango staring at me from one of the stoves. He's fixing me with a stare as if he needs to address me.

"Thanks, Charlotte, let's leave it here. We'll sort it out tomorrow. Getting the manifesto out is more important than the actual cooking. We'll figure something out!" I say, brimming with fake confidence.

She takes her apron off and pats my back gently before leaving. Now it's just Mango here, and he hasn't moved for the past few minutes.

"What?" I ask, slightly irritated. "What, dude?"

"Meow," he begins, "You've lost your wit, bitch."

I feel insulted and head towards him, towering over his tiny body. Maybe I want to intimidate him. He doesn't flinch, though. His eyes get distracted for a second, but then return, staring.

"Meow, I see you still have some fight in you. That's good." He says as he licks his paw.

"So what if I have fight, if that's all I can do?"

"Meow, crouch please. PsPs," he says, and I conform. He slaps me across the face, making sure not to scratch me. "When the apocalypse happened, I had to listen to your sarcastic musings and ironies." He moves his paw under my chin, slightly elevating it. "No matter how much catnip we consumed, meow, you still had some shit to say or mock, meow."

I nod and lower my gaze. He raises my chin again.

"Meow, bitch. An apocalypse didn't kill your creativity and wit, meow. How does a bland man like Burlington do it?"

I pondered Mango's words for a second, and they made sense. He always made sense somehow. Like a furry angel over my shoulder, constantly guiding me towards the light.

"You're right, Mango," I say, fired up. "Fuck that

bland man."

"Meow, fuck him. If he were a jelly pouch, he would be the generic supermarket one. Bland."

"Yeah— if the Black Pyramids were a meal, they would be a cold, boiled, unseasoned potato!"

"Meow! Go bitch go!"

Sophie walks in, disturbed by all the noise. Mango shoots out into the night.

"You okay, Dom?"

I turn around with confidence.

"Better than okay, Sophie, I fucking have it."

The morning is upon us, and as I step out of the tent, the whole commune is outside, cheering me on. They form a nice corridor at the end of which, Charlotte awaits, and I feel like I'm the bride walking down the aisle. Sophie gives me a kiss, "You got this," she tells me. Gerrard waits further down the line. I stop to speak to him as the cheers continue behind me.

"Website good to go?" I ask.

"All good. Chris has the books."

He hugs me and says they will all cheer from home.

"Watch out for the surprise meals," I say, winking.

I move through the crowd, waving presidentially, and arrive at Chris, who hands me a box.

"50 books— the most we could print on short notice."

I open the box to check them.

"Bro," I say, "What's this? They messed up the title."

The book's title is now **WHAT TO EAT AFTER THY APOCALYPSE.** Chris looks at it, unimpressed.

"So what? Makes it sound Shakespearian," he says with a smile. True, after all, who cares? Printing companies went through the same apocalypse. To still have them around is a blessing. *To print with typos or not to print at all. That is the question.*

As I join Charlotte at the end of the catwalk, I see Patience waving outside her house/campaign headquarters. "Get'em, and make sure to season the food!" she shouts.

"Ready?" I ask Charlotte. She is. I'll carry the box of books while she drags a cart full of ingredients. As we make our way out, the cheers intensify, and I hear Sophie shouting from behind.

"Dom, wait!"

I turn to see her running towards me. When she arrives, she catches her breath for one second before pulling out a whisk.

"I know it was a dream," she says. "But maybe it means something."

I start laughing. "You've got to say the phrase, Soph."

She smiles and entertains me. "Take this," she says as she passes me the whisk, "and give these people hope!"

I take it and kiss her goodbye. I wave to the crowd once more as we leave the commune.

Cookfest is held in Trafalgar Square, and the arena is packed with people from all over London. As we make our way through the crowds, we find some organisers who give us our badges and show us towards the contest area. Out of the corner of my eye, I spot, in passing, some Black Pyramids in paramilitary uniforms dispersed through the crowd like sniffer dogs. Charlotte has a spring in her step. She's yet to know my plan, but I doubt she'll complain. Ultimately, the election is more important than any accolades. Arriving in the contest area, I wave at Chef Gomes of Camden.

"Dom!" he greets me, taking off his cooking gloves. I salute him and, without a beat, get to the point in a lower voice.

"I have these books that I need your help with," I say, pointing towards the box I've left by his cooking station. "I've seen some Pyramids in the crowds, and I've got a feeling they have their eyes on me."

He looks through the crowd and spots them himself. "I see. What is it?"

I hug him, trying to avoid the soldiers' gaze, whispering, "My manifesto. I need it shared with all chefs who do not support the Pyramids to take back to their community." I shake his hand, wishing him "Good luck!" loudly but whispering as I leave, "Time is of the essence, Chef. Share them today if you can."

He nods as I join Charlotte, who's setting up our table. Next to me is Chef Murakami from Hoxton, a famous sushi master who was born in Japan but bred in London. I greet her respectfully and walk around the table, helping Charlotte unpack. The contest has been set up in a circle formation, with a camera in the middle of it, I assume for ease of transition between tables. Right across from me on the far end is a man I do not recognise in a black kimono. Tall, slender and meticulous in his placements on the table.

The crowd's cheers grow as Gordon Ramsay makes his way out to the contest area, waving to people and going at his well-known fast pace, saluting each of the contestants. He stops at me.

"Blimey, Dominic. What a pleasure."

I am star-struck. So is Charlotte. We grew up watching Chef Ramsay. I recover before it becomes awkward and shake his hand.

"Weren't you in Malta, sir?"

"I am everywhere, kid," he says, making his way to Murakami.

The broadcast is about to start with everything set up and the live crew confirming the event is good to go. There is a large screen covering the National Gallery where the live feed is presented, and various supporters are shown randomly, reminiscent of events back during the pandemic. I spot Gerrard and Mrs Patel at some point; every 5 seconds, the feed refreshes. Chef Ramsay makes his way to the centre in front of the camera. The crew give him the green light, and the event is underway.

"Economic crisis. Political crisis. Apocalypse. What do all

three have in common?"

He takes a swift break to amplify momentum.

"People. Need. To. Eat." Crowds cheer, and some fireworks are set off as the cameras follow them.

"We've gathered chefs from all the London settlements for a cook-off. Some have cooked for their communes, others started new restaurants, but they all had one thing that kept them going. Passion for food. Ladies and gentlemen, let's meet the contestants."

Chef Ramsay goes around speaking to each chef and arrives at me.

"Hi! I'm Dominic Hargraves, and this is Charlotte Burns. We represent the Commune of Hounslow, and today, we will show how food brings people together."

"Excellent," says Ramsay as he addresses the camera. "Some of us might know Dom from *What to Eat During the Apocalypse*, a cookbook written during the events that shall not be forgotten. Do you have any recipes from the book here today, Dom?"

I shake my head and respond cryptically, "New times call for new recipes, Gordon."

The crowds cheer, and I feel a connection to the public. They are cheering for me loudly, some even carry placards with my name, and it's clear that my past work has made people aware of what I stand for. Perhaps my plan today will draw even more attention to our campaign despite all the tricks the Black Pyramids put together. Gordon turns to the chef in the kimono.

"I'm Chef Worcestershire the Second. Today, I will remind people that class is not a condition but a choice. I represent the future of the city. The Black Pyramids."

Whilst some boos can be heard from the crowd, there is a very large contingent of Black Pyramid supporters shouting that anthem.

"Hail, hail to the rising light,

Where the peaks are clear and the future's bright,

Order guides us through the night,

For the Pyramid, we stand and fight!"

Once all the contestants have been presented, the contest is on, and I quickly explain my plans to Charlotte. She initially seems disheartened, but then agrees that this is a good moment to fight back.

"Fuck it, let's mock them," she says with a growing smile on her face.

We work together effortlessly. Leaves, cucumbers, and olives all thrown in, tossed. We arrange the top nicely, and the clock starts buzzing. The crowd erupts in another cheer.

There are some great recipes before our turn: soups, bruschetta, rice-based dishes, couscous—the usuals. Impressive showings. Chef Ramsay arrives at my table.

"Here, Chef, we have the *Order and Chaos Salad*."

Chef Ramsay uses a fork to pick up the salad, but finds it difficult.

"This, Dom— it's messy. I expected better standards."

"Sorry, Chef," I reply. "This is a salad where order reigns on the surface, but chaos is inevitable once you dig in." I can sense some applause from the crowd as Chef Ramsay shakes his head, disappointed, and moves on. I can see some messages on the live stream, as watchers are starting to catch on. "*LOL*," says one, while another reads, "*This is exactly what Burlington promises us!*"

Arriving at Chef Worcestershire, the Second, the camera shows an impressive starter.

"This is the *Sphere of Pleasure*, as I call it," It looks like a lump to me.

"It has foie gras and a dash of caviar inside. Saffron

rice supports the whole construction, showing that grand things can be achieved with some control and discipline."

Ramsay tastes it and is truly impressed, muttering many sounds of pleasure.

"My god. Amazing. Excellent. Well done."

I sense that my plan wasn't as original as I thought. I shouldn't have expected otherwise. Burlington would use this, just like me, as another platform to promote his ideology. And to be honest, it looks delicious. Worcestershire looks at me menacingly as if he's trying to show off.

Ramsay and the public judge the contest. He gives a grade from one to ten, and people on the live stream give individual grades depending on each dish's popularity. The maximum you can get in a round is 20. Worcestershire, the Second, is first. I'm seventh, with the public giving me 8 points to Ramsay's 2.

The second round kicks off. This is the mains section, and this should be my centrepiece. This is the one that got Charlotte excited, too. She starts boiling the rice and chopping some vegetables while I deal with the rest of the meal. I see Worcestershire across from me, calm and collected, each move seemingly calculated and executed precisely. He doesn't even have a helper, which is a testament to his self-belief. The clock buzzes, and the round is over. We are done just in time, and behind us, I can hear some murmurs and people whispering in astonishment.

As usual, Chef Ramsay goes around showing and tasting delicious recipes. Lamb Tagine, Donburi, Feijoada. Gordon is living my dream right now. He arrives at my table, and the camera zooms in on it.

"Uhm, wow," he says, excitedly shaking his head. "This is interesting!"

The camera shows my pyramid with a rice base, rising in layers of different grains to hold a piece of beef fillet at the very top.

"It seems a bit impractical, though grandiose in presentation," says Chef Ramsay as he forks through the grains.

"I call this the *Pyramid of Geezer*, Gordon," I say as the murmurs grow, and I can hear disapproving noises from the Black Pyramid supporters. "It is a pyramid built on the backs of the grain that props up the meal. The grain, I guess, would symbolise your working man."

"Hm," he says, "Impractical, but delicious. Good, thank you."

With crowds cheering again, the live stream is flooded with messages of support.

"I can't believe it— Go, Dom!"

"Fuck the Pyramids!"

"You can't go against the grain!"

I look at Charlotte, and she grins at me. Through the crowds, though, you can feel the anger of the Black Pyramids rising.

Chef Worcestershire finishes the round with "*The Golden Lamb*", a succulent shank dipped in gold mashed potatoes, showing London as the centre of the UK, in all of its riches."

Gordon loves it and can't help but give it full marks for this round. But the public has tipped the balance, scoring Worcestershire low and me with full marks. I'm fired up to finish strongly. I'm currently third, while Worcestershire the Second is first.

Ahead of the last round, the transmission is taken over by commercial breaks, reminiscent of older times. As the event is sponsored by and streamed with the help of Vylan Tusk, all the adverts are for his companies.

One after another, they roll on, with no appeal to the general public. They are nothing but vanity projects aimed at boosting a man's ego who likely had few friends growing up but plenty of money. I can't help but notice that each commercial shared has subliminal references to the Black Pyramids. A pyramid with an electric car sitting on top, one for a spaceship with the boldened text of **ORDER** and **PROGRESS** launching from the tip of a black pyramid.

With the final round underway, Charlotte and I are hyper-focused on finishing strongly. Sweat builds up on my forehead, but in between doing her duties, she finds time to wipe it off with a rag. With the whisk Sophie gave me, I whip that cream to perfection . Time's up.

"That's it, folks!" says Ramsay. "The last round!"

Anticipation builds as he walks around the tables tasting each dessert. He arrives at my table yet again, raising his eyebrows.

"This is *Burlington's Broken Pavlova*," I say as raucous laughter breaks out in the crowd. "It is a fragile, crumbling creation, much like Burlington's vision for London. It may look sweet and tempting on the outside, but it's sour and bitter to the taste."

The Pyramids hate the sound of it. Gordon hates the

taste of it.

"I see what you're trying to do, but my god, does it taste horrible." He winks at me before moving on.

Last, yet again, is Worcestershire, presenting a fine chocolate mousse. "This is called the *Amousse Bouche*."

A voice from the crowd replies, "Amousse Douche!" to the visible fury of the Pyramid supporters. I turn around and salute my brother in puns, appreciating his effort. However, Worcestershire continues, undeterred, "It shows that the finest things in life take patience, care and strong initiative." Gordon tastes it and falls to his knees. "Fucking amazing. Well done," he says, gesticulating in excitement.

As usual, Gordon is voting as expected. He isn't an idealist; he is a famous chef. He can only judge food. And he loved everything Worcestershire presented, understandably. It comes down to the vote from the public. Charlotte and I hold hands as the numbers appear on the screen. The crowd hushes in anticipation.

I get top marks. Leaving me joint first with Worcestershire as the public erupts in excitement, to my joint winners' disappointment. Gordon, however, can have only one winner, so he will go around to the other contestants, having them pick a winner. As he passes, there is only one winner from each Chef: *"Dom!"* I am first and Worcestershire the Second is second. The crowd is delirious, and I can't believe it; I see Gerrard, Sophie, and Mrs Patel cheering from the commune on the screen. I have tears in my eyes.

"Ladies and gentlemen, the public and the chefs have decided! We have a winner. Dom of Hounslow," he says as confetti erupts in the contest area.

Chefs start clapping, walking towards us to join in on the group picture. On the screen, messages of congratulations pour in. The crowd is still roaring, the confetti drifting through the air. But something feels…off. Worcestershire is on the phone, nodding. Then he puts it away. A hush spreads.

Then, the sound of a gunshot breaks the celebration abruptly.

I jump towards Charlotte to help her duck under the table. The crowds start dispersing, screaming and shouting. Everyone rushes away from the arena, apart from the Black Pyramids, who are now marching towards us. Charlotte is frozen, watching the whole scene unfold, so I grab her by the vest, and we start running through the chaos, dodging people as they scramble in all directions. Chef Gomes jumps in front of us and asks us to follow him through a path out of the main square. As we turn the corner, I can see a bloodied Gordon Ramsay behind me, shouting "Blimey!" and thudding to the ground. It feels as if he took a bullet for me.

We manage to get in a black cab, and I shout for the driver to go. I see the depleted, worn-out army battalion slowly making its way towards Trafalgar Square. The driver hits the pedal, and we leave with tyres squeaking, shocked but unscathed. If they can't handle losing a cooking contest, what's going to happen if they lose the election?

BOILING POINT

Having returned safely to Hounslow, the commune rallies behind us, and Chris sets up a system of patrols around our area. "Non-violent deterrence," he calls it. Charlotte is still shaken, days after the event and the tension in the commune is palpable. While everyone is proud of my performance at *Cookfest*, the events at the end made everyone fearful of the prospects of a Black Pyramid win.

Gerrard, who maintained optimism "based on data", is the only one unshaken by it all.

"Check this out," he says, showing me a graph whilst passing me letters from supporters. He reads one out loud. *"We are all behind you in Primrose. Fuck the Douche."*

I check the data. It all looks promising.

"That's really encouraging, mate. How's the website doing?"

I turn my eyes to the map, scouting for a location for a rally, whilst he clicks a few times and turns the screen back towards me.

"Pretty good," he says, showing me another graph with a massive spike the first couple of days after *Cookfest*. "We're getting thousands of views daily. I even switched the IP to the United States, so it's more difficult to take down."

"Smart stuff Gerr, thank you mate."

I find an area in West London that seems suitable. I look at Chris, who occasionally glances out the window as if he's checking for any sign of trouble. "Chris, what do you think about this spot?" I say as I show him Syon Park.

He inspects it carefully and tells me it's a bad idea.

"Why?"

"The whole idea of a rally is dangerous," he replies, returning to the window and staring off into the distance. "It doesn't matter where; they have it out for you since you humiliated them publicly."

Sophie agrees with Chris. Seeing the scenes on the live stream was traumatising for her, and she wanted me to stop campaigning. When we returned that afternoon, she wouldn't let me out of her sight, following me around the commune.

I am too committed now and want to see this through. I am tired of being chased around and bullied into submission. Every day, members of the commune come to offer their support. We print more books, and people go in pairs to different parts of London, handing books to people keen on opposing the Pyramids, carrying my words. They go door knocking every day, spreading my message. I jokingly called them *Dom's Witnesses* once when addressing them and delegating areas, to the disapproval of Patience.

We decide to push ahead with the rally three days before the election, posting about it on our website. I plead with Chris and Sophie to agree with the idea of Syon Park.

"Fine," he concludes, "But you'll have personal armed guards. I'll lead them."

I hate the thought of it but see the necessity.

Since the shootout at *Cookfest*, Chris's military discipline has been on high alert. He goes on runs every morning and evening, does push-ups whenever he has a few minutes off, and even stops vaping every five minutes, allowing himself a reward vape every hour.

It's the night before the rally, and we're all in the mess hall, enjoying our meal and trying to muster as much energy as possible for the day ahead. When the doors open halfway through our meal, a familiar face appears.

"Captain!" I shout, full of joy at the sight of Fowler. He walks in with a few armed soldiers.

"A birdie told me," he says, smiling at Chris, "that there's a considerable threat to your life. Now, I can't let that happen." I get up and shake his hand.

"What about the army not getting involved, Cap?"

He looks around at his soldiers, all smiling mischievously.

"Well," he says, smirking, "We are technically on leave." He walks towards me, putting his hand on my shoulder paternally. "Now, I don't suppose you guys have a few spare rifles lying around?"

"Yes, we fecking do!" says an excited Chris to the cheers of Hounsies.

I hug Fowler and look at his young soldiers, thankful for their support. "Fancy some bhajis?" I say extending a basket of some of the freshest bhajis in London, courtesy of Mrs Patel.

As we eat and chat more with Fowler, we understand that the army is divided and on its knees.

"Some actually side with the Pyramids now. Most of these lads are about following orders, Dom, and they see them as the likely winners."

He reveals that before *Cookfest*, Pyramid-bought generals ensured that there was not much security around the event. This ultimately led to the death of three, caught between the shooting and the stampede that followed, Chef Ramsay amongst them. He tells me Burlington was seething at what happened, and he basically put a price tag on my head. Surprisingly, he still wants the elections to go ahead.

The calm before the storm is setting in. In our tent, I wrap my arms tightly around Sophie in bed as she has a moment of anxiety. Mango shows up and decides to curl up against her. Stroking Mango, she tells me she is worried about the future, should the Pyramids win.

"What will happen to you? To us?" she asks with fear in her voice.

I kiss the back of her neck. "We pack a bag tomorrow," I say, trying to reassure her. "We hit the M25, and we make our way to Dover. Cross the channel if we must." I start stroking her hair gently. "I will not allow danger to come near you."

"Meow Bitch."

"Or you, Mango," I add, realising he feels left out.

She pushes up against me, seeking my warmth. We fall asleep to the sound of Mango purring.

·····

We are somewhere on the Spanish coast. I watch Sophie tanning on the balcony, the shapes of her body drawing my attention. I approach her, and she hands me an empty glass.

"Is there more Sangria?"

"There is not. I'll head to the shop to get some."

"You're an angel," she says, smiling.

I cross the road to the shop and speak to the shopkeeper in broken Spanish.

"Buenos dias. One des sangria. Por favour."

The shopkeeper heads towards the fridge when I spot the headlines of *El Mundo,* a Spanish newspaper.

Las Pirámides Negras han comenzado las deportaciones

Oddly, I understood it fully.

The shopkeeper returns and hands me an ice-cold carton of cheap Sangria. I ask him for the newspaper, too.

"Gracias," I say.

"De nada."

I'm walking back to our villa and spot Mango sitting in the shade of a palm tree.

"Meow, *puta*," he greets me.

I walk inside to find Sophie tied up on the floor, with two men in balaclavas by her side. Her mouth is gagged, and her makeup is running down her cheeks.

"Que quieres?" I ask, panicking. "Yo tengo money, not mucho, mas you can have it!"

One of the men makes a step towards me. He is twice my size.

"I'll tell you what we want, lad." He says this while I notice his gold Black Pyramid necklace shining, blinding me. With one hand, he strikes me from the side, and I fall thudding to the ground. Still tied up, Sophie's cries and pleadings echo in my head. My vision becomes blurry and fades out.

"Thought you'd get away with it, huh?" the man says before I pass out.

.....

I wake up with a sheen of sweat all over my body. I turn

and do not see Sophie. A brief moment of panic overwhelms me. My heart is in my throat, and I want to freeze, but sitting still is impossible. I step outside, and the commune is still there. Sophie is talking to Edna. She spots me and makes her way to me.

"Good morning," she says, kissing me on the cheek. "You kept moving a lot last night. Was it a bad dream?"

"It was," I say. "Thankfully, just that."

People start walking onto the street and speaking to neighbours. I overhear them saying, "Is it working for you?"

I can't help my curiosity and ask them, "Sorry, guys. What's the problem?"

"The internet," one says. "We can't access it."

At Patience's house, Gerrard scrambles to find a solution whilst we wait on the couch.

"Tusk?" Mrs Patel asks while I shrug my shoulders.

"It can't be," I can hear Gerrard nearing a tantrum. "These motherfuckers!" is followed by the sound of something breaking.

Chris scouts the surroundings from the window.

When he sees something outside, he rushes out. "Help! Help!" can be heard. I follow.

Ola, one of the young lads in the commune, makes his way through the gates with a bullet wound in his shoulder. Chris helps him inside, and a crowd starts gathering. Some inside, others peeking through the windows.

"Place him on the table!" shouts Patience as she's trying to clear the room. Joanne, a former nurse, makes her way to the front.

"Bring me something to put pressure on his shoulder." Mrs Patel scrambles for a tea rag.

"They are coming," Ola says in between trying to catch his breath. "Argh! Is it stuck in?" he shouts in pain.

"The bullet went through," Joanne says. "I should be able to stitch him up."

Charlotte offers to fetch medical supplies for Joanne. By the time she starts treating his wounds, Chris is already outside, rallying people to take defensive positions. Fowler orders his men to be the first line of defence outside the commune.

Chris steps inside the house briefly. "Dom, we need

to get you out now."

I look at Sophie, and panic is all over her face. Ola's screams penetrate the room. I put my arms around Sophie's waist and look her in the eyes.

"Hey, hey, look here," I tell her as she slowly lifts her gaze. "Grab Mango, pack our bag and get ready by the tent. If they push in, go to Hounslow West underground."

"I'll be with you," says Mrs Patel, sensing that Sophie might need help. I thank her with a quick nod.

"Hey," I tell Sophie again. "We fought these fascists before, and we won." I gently wipe a sole tear running down her cheek. "If not, Dover, yeah?" She nods, and Mrs Patel takes her away, up the road to our tent.

I go outside to find complete chaos. People are already leaving, and some are heading to the underground, which is a few yards away. As the sound of a rhythmic march nearing the commune intensifies, the atmosphere is thick with anticipation and dread.

One shot hits a barrel. Another one smashes a window. They are here.

Chris huddles behind a cart, his breath shallow, fingers fumbling for the last bullets in his pouch. His hands are shaking, whether from adrenaline or fear, I can't tell. I crawl on my stomach through the dust; I can taste gunpowder. The smell of smoke fills my nostrils.

"Here," I mutter, tossing a handful of bullets his way. They clatter against the stone, and he grabs them with shaking fingers. A loud crack rings out from the front gate as the Black Pyramid forces surge forward, their boots hammering against the ground in unison like an unstoppable tide.

"They're pushing to the gate!" Chris shouts, shoving the bullets into his rifle and aiming over the cart. "Dom, we can't hold them too long. You need to go!"

Fowler staggers into the square, a smear of blood streaked across his cheek, his face twisted in a mixture of pain and fury. He wipes it away with his sleeve, shouting to his men, but I can barely hear him over the screams and gunfire.

Then, the world goes silent.

The shooting stops so suddenly it's as though someone flicked a switch, cutting off the chaos. My ears ring from the silence, and the stench of gunpowder hangs thick in the air. I press my back against the cart and risk a glance toward Chris. He's wide-eyed, his breath coming in short bursts as if waiting for something to shatter the stillness.

"Get up," he says, motioning toward me. My body feels stiff as I rise to my knees, and my senses buzz. What is going on? Have they pulled back?

But as I step forward, something glints in the air—a metallic clatter as it lands by my feet. A grenade. It takes a few seconds, but a mushroom of green gas forms when it explodes. I fall to the ground, coughing. The gas rushes at me like a wall, a toxic green cloud that grips my lungs, burning as I gasp for air. I drop to my knees, coughing so hard it feels like my chest might tear open.

Then, strong arms haul me up from the ground. It's Byron, with a rag around his mouth. He's coughing, too, his face sweaty from the effort, but his grip on my shoulder is ironclad as he drags me forward through the choking fog.

"I got you, Dom...keep moving!" His voice is ragged, as though each word takes everything out of him. The gas wraps around us, thickening, and no matter how fast Byron pulls, the cloud lingers, creeping closer like it's hunting us. Each step I take is like dragging my feet through a muddy swamp, pulling me back.

I hear Chris shouting somewhere behind us, but it's all muted, distant. I glance up through tear-blurred eyes and see him running toward us.

Then, a crack. A gunshot rings out.

Suddenly, Byron stumbles, his hand slipping from my shoulder. I stop moving, my breath catching in my throat as I look down in horror. He's lying on the ground, his body jerking. They got him.

"No!" The word comes out as a whisper. I try to kneel beside him, to reach for him, but my legs give out beneath me, and the gas makes it hard to see.

Chris emerges through the thick of it, all masked up, dragging me away just as Byron's body goes limp. The gas is closing in, taking over each road in the commune. He hoists me onto his back. I glance over my shoulder, my heart breaking as I watch Byron fade from view, swallowed by the toxic mist.

"Almost there," Chris mutters, his voice thick with exhaustion. We push on, the green cloud at our heels, but it no longer matters.

We're underground at Hounslow West, and there's a large group around us, all with a terrified look on their face. Chris leans me against the wall. He throws his mask at the wall, cussing. I can hear Sophie screaming as I fade in and out of consciousness. Joanne is rushing over alongside Patience. A small group gathers around me.

I wake up in an upright position with Sophie sleeping on my shoulder. My thigh is wrapped in a makeshift dressing, and a couple of our guys patrol the platform while everyone else sleeps. I greet them with a nod, and they smile, happy to see me awake.

Around the station, I see old markings and children's drawings on the side of the rail—a living memory of where we started from and where we've eventually returned to. I see Gerrard coming from the tunnel, his face illuminated by the laptop. When he spots me, his steps speed up. "Dom," he whispers, "Good to have you back, mate."

"Good to be back," I whisper, trying not to wake Sophie up. "Where's Mango?" I ask.

He points towards the roof of a vending machine a few feet away, where Mango is curled up next to Bowie, fast asleep. I let out a sigh of relief.

"Dom," Gerrard continues. "I've walked down the tunnels; there is one spot where I get a signal for the internet."

My eyes light up. "The website?" I ask.

"Still there. They tried to shut it down whilst attacking us, but I've managed to reroute it yet again."

I know what I need to do now.

I slowly get up and gently put Sophie down, managing not to wake her. With one hand firmly on his shoulder for support, I go with Gerrard. We find the spot, and with the signal at full strength, I ask Gerrard to help me record a video.

The red button now flashing, I begin.

"Londoners, we've stood at the edge before, and every time, our strength has pulled us back. Today, I saw brave men and women stand against tyranny, against fascism. I saw Byron give his own life. But this fight isn't over. We owe it to him, to Chef Ramsay and the others, to push back. To fight for a London where freedom isn't just a word. Today, it was the Commune of Hounslow. Tomorrow, it could be you. We can't let this happen. Not again."

Gerrard has gathered video footage from people's phones and begins uploading it onto our website, nervously biting his nails.

For once, I'm not afraid. Death is just around the corner, one way or another, so why live in fear? I feel ready for anything that may come. Should they win, I will sail from Dover to France and build my resistance there.

I look to Gerrard and his belief in our mission. I admire Patience and Mrs Patel's care, Sophie's love, and Chris's loyalty. On the platforms, the Hounsies lick their wounds and ready themselves again to build community in the face of division.

Family. This is why we do what needs to be done. A bullet may kill a man, letting his body thud on the very ground he stands on, but it will never kill what he stands for.

The upload is complete.

THE FINAL COURSE

Today is supposed to be the day of the rally, but it finds us hiding in the underground. As soon as the gates open to the station, people pour in, bringing supplies, food and most importantly, armed men to help patrol outside. My video was seen by thousands of people, and word from other settlements is that people have started rebelling against the Black Pyramids, and fighting has been going on overnight. I see Mango chasing Bowie through the tunnels like in the old days, and Mrs Patel helping a couple of women move supplies. Edna is resting against the wall, and I notice the bags under her red-rimmed eyes as she stares into the abyss.

"Y'alright?"

She looks up at me. "Not really. I feel guilty." For once, she doesn't indulge in our usual exchange, devoid of meaning.

"For?" I ask as I crouch slowly beside her.

"Byron," she replies. "All this time, I pointed fingers at him."

I put my arm around her. "We've all done things we normally wouldn't." She shakes her head, her face riddled with remorse.

"Hey Edna, where are you from?" I ask in a light tone, trying to change the topic.

"Ukraine." She says, attempting a smile.

I get up in pain. I move across the platform where Sophie is speaking to Gerrard as he shows her something on the laptop.

"Look at this," he says, handing me the device. For once, Tusk's thoughts are at the bottom, and a message from Burlington takes the first page.

Dear Londoners. I profusely apologise for images or stories that have used our name over the past few days. I sincerely apologise to Dominic and the commune of Hounslow for yesterday's events. This was not a Black Pyramid action, but of some supporters who have since been caught and will face the dire consequences of their actions. We stand for order, not violence. For the pain and destruction their actions have caused, I vow here, before you, to actively help rebuild Hounslow and support its residents.

It then carried on with usual political statements and

vote-pleading.

"They are scared, Dom," Gerrard says, taking the laptop from my hands. "The tide is turning on them already."

His enthusiasm is evident. I try to temper it. "Let's not forget what it cost us," I say as I turn towards a still-grieving Edna. "There are 24 hours to go. We either win this and can begin to repair our community, or we lose and get used to the smell of the underground again."

Patience descends the stairs and sees me. There's warmth in her eyes. "White boy, come with me."

I walk up the stairs, leaning on her shoulders for support. Each step feels a bit less painful. Or that might be the morphine Joanne gave me.

I get outside the tube station, and I'm immediately faced by hundreds of people all cheering and chanting: *Dom! Dom! Dom!*

I raise my hand to salute them as they approach me. It's a clear summer day, and the sun radiates across the high street. I see a baker approaching me with a coffee and a croissant. The atmosphere is hopeful. I take a bite of that warm, buttery pastry, and all of a sudden, yesterday's pain is turned into excitement for tomorrow. Or, again, it might be the morphine. I raise my half-bitten croissant in the air and shout.

"Tomorrow, we kick the Pyramids out!"

The crowd erupts and starts chanting, *"Fuck the Pyramids!"*

The day of the election is finally upon us, and messages from all over London say they have voted for me. Fearing any possible attacks, we remain underground despite the overwhelming protection shown by other communities. Our new campaign headquarters are now the old survival headquarters, the supply room. Being here brings so many flashbacks—the first time Patience knocked me over, Mr Patel making biryani, and the arrival of Fowler. It would be almost fun were it not for the dread of what may await tomorrow.

The internet is available all day, as promised by Tusk, and our signal has been repaired surprisingly quickly; we are reading news from across London. It seems like the turnout is higher than ever, with online voting running smoothly. We are watching international news, too; it is so weird seeing my face on CNN or Mexican cable news. From what we can gather, it seems that the international community is behind our cause. An in-memoriam documentary about Gordon Ramsay is running on

PBS, linking it to the current election and the levels of political violence seen.

"I think we're going to do it!" Says Sophie, filled with hope. I smile back and try to contain my emotions.

Out of nowhere, Mrs Patel walks in with a large, steaming pot. Behind her, Chris comes in with several bowls and hands us one each.

"What's this?" I ask curiously.

"Biryani," responds Mrs Patel, placing a large scoop in my bowl. The smell is sublimely fragrant and aromatic, and each bite gives me more strength than whatever morphine Joanne could pump into me. Jamie Foxx appears at the door, Chris throws him a bone, and he darts off into the tunnels with it.

"Can you make sure," says Mrs Patel in between bites, "That you lower the price of Basmati, Mr Mayor?"

We all start laughing, and for once in the past few weeks, we find genuine relief. It might be Mrs Patel's concern for the price of rice. Or maybe this recipe got me thinking of Mr Patel and his sacrifice for the cause in the early days, or Byron's a few days ago. Perhaps these walls have seen it all—terror, hope, love, community—none of which we ever forgot, no matter how things change around us. I look at Sophie and catch her eyes. "I love you," I whisper.

The evening is fast approaching, and Fowler makes his way down the platform.

"Are you ready?" he asks.

I turn around from rubbing Mango's belly to see him surrounded by a few men.

"Ready for?" I ask, confused.

"Results night, you fool. Sorry, Mr Mayor."

I laugh. "I thought they would announce them tomorrow. Do I have to be somewhere?"

"Yes," he says as he asks one of his men to step forward, presenting a dry-cleaned suit. "With online voting, results are available in one hour. You have to be at the Council."

Sophie grabs my hand and seems excited. I look at the suit, unimpressed. It reminds me of my office job from before the apocalypse. I hand it back to Fowler.

"I'll take an apron instead."

Fowler smiles and makes his way to the armoured vehicles waiting outside. I turn to the group of people, all looking towards me now.

"Go," says Patience, full of hope. "Win this for us. We'll be there to cheer for you."

The roads are packed with British flags, and people wave at me as an army convoy takes me to the Council. I have hope as we drive through this beautiful, fractured city. The Palace is brimming with guests, and as I walk into the main chambers, the chatter grinds to a halt. All eyes are on me. I see the Duke of Primrose Hill making way and lowering his gaze. A corridor forms towards the stage where General Sobinski is waiting next to Burlington and some representatives from the revived Conservatives and Labour parties. As I drag my leg across the room, Burlington walks off the stage and offers me a hand in a supposedly nice gesture.

"Come here, Dom, it's so good to see you're okay!" he says with a smile, in front of the press. We shake hands, and the camera flashes. This moment is what he lived for. I look him dead in the eyes and whisper to him.

"If I win this, you're dead." Reciprocating the same fake smirk he gave me. I get up onto the stage, and in the front row, I see Vylan Tusk smiling and waving at me. What a prick.

"Silence, please!" the general instructs as journalists

and guests take their seats. The lights on the stage are blinding me, and I feel like passing out. This whole moment feels surreal, and I can feel each breath in my chest and the rush of blood to my head. "Liam Cuthwell from the Conservatives, 52,149 votes." Some scattered applause can be heard. "Veronica Fergusson, Labour, 175,222 votes." Some more scattered applause and cheers are heard from the room.

"James Burlington. Black Pyramids. 1,700,802 votes."

Half of the room erupts. Cheers and applause—his supporters know they have it. My stomach turns. Burlington tilts his head at me, a smug little nod like he's already celebrating.

"Dominic Hargraves. Commune of Hounslow," announces the General.

The silence stretches on and on. My heart pounds in my ears. "One million..." I hold my breath.

"...eight hundred seventy-five thousand, two hundred and forty-three votes."

The room explodes in the loudest cheer of the night. Burlington dashes off the stage, nodding to Tusk, who follows him. Gerrard, Patience and Sophie hurry into the room and run towards the stage. I smile from ear to ear.

"Congratulations to our new mayor," announces the General, "Dominic Hargraves!"

The room quickly empties of the Black Pyramids. Triumphal music is ringing in the speakers. Sophie jumps onto the stage and hugs me whilst the journalists all have their hands up, awaiting a speech. *Shit. I haven't prepared one.*

I take a deep breath, the microphone screeching slightly as I approach the lectern. I can barely make out the faces in front of me—faces filled with anticipation, hope, and joy. Sophie joins Gerrard and Patience off to the side. I catch her eye. She gives me a small nod, the kind that says, "*You've got this.*"

I grip the edge of the lectern, trying to steady myself. The crowd quiets, and the room is eagerly awaiting my speech. I clear my throat, and I decide to speak from the heart.

"Londoners..." I start. My voice is a little shaky, but I push through. "Today, we've done something extraordinary."

The room goes completely silent.

I scan the crowd. Some are nodding. Some are still on edge, not daring to believe what has happened. I get it. After everything we've been through, it's hard to trust that something good may come out of it.

"This victory," I continue, "our victory, isn't just about defeating the Black Pyramids or standing up against their violence. It's about something bigger than any one of us. It's about hope."

I pause, the word lingering in the air like a fragile thing, and I feel the weight of it. The crowd is still listening, still waiting, so I keep going. A few scattered camera flashes can be heard.

"We've all lost so much. People we loved, homes, lives that we thought would always be there. And this city? It's not the same as it used to be. We're not the same as we used to be. But you know what we haven't lost?" I lean in, my voice growing stronger with each word.

"Our fight. We haven't lost the spark inside us that refuses to give up or bow down to anyone who thinks they can take away what's ours."

I glance at Gerrard for a moment. He's beaming, like a proud parent watching his kid score the winning goal in the 90th minute. I look back at the crowd, trying to find faces in the blur of lights and flashes.

"I'm not gonna stand here and tell you this is the end of the fight," I say, my voice growing firmer, "Because it's not. It's the beginning. We've won today, but there will be more challenges, battles, Pyramids, and more seeking to sow division. But I promise you this..."

I pause again, letting the gravity of what I'm about to say sink in.

"As long as I draw breath, I will fight for every one of you. Not as a politician. Not as a mayor. But as one of you," I say, trying to meet the eye of every person in the room. "We will not go back to living in fear. We will not let them decide what our future looks like. London belongs to us."

The crowd starts to stir. I can feel the energy building, the belief starting to set in, but I need to make this real for them.

"They'll try to break us," I continue, "But we will stand together. We've been through hell and back not once but twice. And now, we're going to do more than survive. We're going to thrive."

I straighten up, the pain in my leg forgotten momentarily as the adrenaline takes over.

"This is our city. Our home. And today is the day we take it back!"

The room erupts into cheers, and I take it all in. The noise, the excitement, the relief. My family is here, excited, hopeful, hugging each other. It's overwhelming, but in the best way possible. I step back from the mic, smiling. Sophie rushes over to me, throwing her arms around my neck, and for the first time in what feels like forever, I let myself believe we've actually done it.

As I walk off the stage and exit the chambers, I am welcomed by supporters who've collectively decided to wear the apron as a sign of support. If only Gordon Ramsay was here to witness these scenes. I make a V for victory gesture with my hands. Chris pops out from the crowd and starts spraying me with champagne.

As the wine drips from my hair, I spot something in the distance. A helicopter, rising above the skyline. Not a military one, but one of Tusk's. The blades cut through the sky, slicing through the cheers like a quiet threat. I feel Gerrard at my side, watching it too. Neither of us says anything. We don't have to.

CLEARING THE TABLE

The first few weeks after the election presented plenty of challenges. I was lucky to have the counsel of my friends to keep me right and fair throughout. A few Black Pyramid protests erupted across the city, claiming the election had been stolen, with Burlington giving updates on Tusk's platform and claiming that I had "rigged" it. His protestors tried to storm Buckingham Palace several times but were met with fierce resistance by regular Londoners who wanted to turn the page on this rhetoric. Burlington himself was nowhere to be seen. It was suggested he found refuge in Vylan Tusk's living room, where he would occasionally send updates to a decimated force of the Black Pyramids. Early on, I decided not to take punitive action against its members and tried to win hearts instead. Large numbers of them gave up the balaclavas and masks, but there was still a small, strong contingent of radicalised members trying to wreak havoc on the streets.

"I say we go hard on them and lock them up," Chris would suggest, always ready to get the newly founded Peace Brigade involved. The PB was a new form of policing we'd devised, with rotating numbers of volunteers and clear attributes of ensuring peace rather than inciting violence through authority. The army was always on standby for the more complex outbursts of violence, but most of the time, we tried to reason and help others lay down arms instead of raising our own.

A month into my mayorship, I met with the Prime Minister of the UK in hopes of reintegrating London into the wider country. Our meetings were always warm.

"We missed you," she said whilst on the cusp of agreeing to a period of transition.

"We are stronger together," I said, shaking her hand.

People were genuinely happy. And no one was happier than Mrs Patel when I negotiated a new deal for basic necessities, taking the price of basmati rice down to pre-MBGA levels. Using Gerrard's savviness, we built platforms appealing to worldwide crowdfunding for efforts to rebuild our city. Plenty of investment firms and sharks started circling London once the election ended, offering large sums with small fine print about interest rates.

"Fuck off, you and your WhiteRock," I said to one of the fund managers, coming into my office one day with a big smile and a presentation made by some junior, saying how London's diversity is its strength and how much our values align. My first call with Donald Trump, serving his 6th term as the despot of the US, went along similar lines. "Fuck off, Donnie. No more golf clubs in London."

"Fine. Tariffs for you. Tariffs for all of London," he said before hanging up, severing diplomatic ties.

I decided to organise my first event for the public in the second month. We all needed some relief, and the closest we had had in the last year was *Cookfest*. The newly organised *Ramsay Memorial* would raise the stakes and bring chefs from all over the world, making the competition international and having London as one team. I didn't participate, knowing my fame as a chef was due to circumstance rather than skill. The event brought the first wave of tourists back to London, and among them was Yas, my ex-girlfriend. It was our first get-together since before MBGA, when she decided to leave the country for her own sake. "I'm really proud of you, Dom," she said. We kept it brief so as not to abuse

Sophie's trust and goodwill.

I turned one of the supply rooms in the palace into a space for Mango, with scratching posts all over and an obstacle course to keep him entertained. "Meow, Mayor Bitch," he'd greet me whenever I'd come to check in on him. He allowed Bowie, and, to the complaints of the cleaning staff, Jamie Foxx, to hang out with him there. Some of my video calls with world leaders were slightly embarrassing due to the racket they made.

As the months rolled by, the city began knitting itself back together, like flesh healing after a deep wound. The streets of Camden bustled again, food stalls lining the market with scents of roasted chestnuts, shawarma, and curry drifting through the air. Westminster's shattered windows were replaced with new panes, sunlight streaming like hope finding its way back in.

On the Southbank, artists had returned, painting on easels by the Thames, while a street musician played an old tune on a saxophone, the notes carrying over the river. Once dark and abandoned, the towers of Canary Wharf flickered with light again as businesses returned, cautious but eager to rebuild. I even got to stand in Wembley Stadium, surrounded by 90,000 fans, as my team, Newcastle, battered Arsenal in the FA Cup final—proof that the heart of the city, despite everything, still beat strong.

Professionals who had previously left London due to unaffordable housing were returning as unoccupied villas and flats, held as assets by foreign oligarchs, were given back to the public, raising money for the reconstruction of the city and offering housing stock.

The commune of Hounslow flourished under the guidance of Charlotte.

Mrs Patel opened a restaurant in Mayfair, and the *have-a-lots* loved it. With a change of heart after the election, they started to appreciate the benefits of a diverse society again. The biryani was a top seller, and for good reason.

Patience started running an organisation to help immigrants and those recently made homeless reintegrate into our new society. The new housing stock required careful consideration and planning, ensuring the integration of those not born here with the local communities. I went to one of their meetings once and saw her chairing the committee with so much pride and energy.

"Seems like you found your purpose," I told her.

"There's much to do, Dom," she said, focused and determined.

Chris opened a vape shop in central London, building a Hall of Fame of vapes and charging tourists to enter a part of the shop called the *Museum of Blue Razz*. He would occasionally come by my office, bringing burgers or some fried chicken, and we would play a game of cards where he would always use his strategic brain to his advantage. He ran the Peace Brigade as a passion project and would always consult with me on big initiatives and vice versa; I always sought his military experience as a guide in handling protests or trouble.

Captain Fowler was his second in command, helping him set it up for the first few months, after which he decided to retire. "What are you going to do now?" I asked him at his retirement gala, attended by many from the commune.

"Well, with the roads opening up, I'm considering taking a caravan across Europe. See the old continent." He said with excitement in his eyes.

Gerrard was my second in command and my best friend. Given the big challenges ahead with integration into wider networks and the growing cybercrime threat, he would end up overseeing the Internet and the communications side of governing. One of his first initiatives as Internet czar was to outlaw Vylan Tusk's platform. "We can't have freedom of speech at the expense of other people's freedom of safety," he said in a public broadcast. Tusk went into a frenzy, tirade after tirade of calling London the Gestapo and other names, showing his true colours to the public.

One day, I was walking with Gerrard in Regent's Park. It was a sunny spring day. Swans were flying across the lake, and people were laying out picnic blankets and opening bottles of Prosecco, which was affordable again.

"We've got an offer from the EU to help us rebuild fibre optics across the city. This would restore coverage to about 99%," he said, excited.

"Sounds good," I said as we kept walking.

"Something on your mind?" he asked, stopping in his tracks.

I looked at him and told him I was proud of him and our journey through all this.

"Wouldn't have it any other way," he said.

"Hey, nerd?" I added as I rummaged through my

pockets and showed him a wedding ring.

He acted surprised, taking a step back. "Aw, no, Dom. Man, I love you, but not like that."

I laughed. "No, you idiot. D'you want to be my best man?"

Of course, he did. I just needed to make sure Sophie was still keen on marrying me.

One evening, after making her favourite pasta dish, Cacio e Pepe, we were all alone on the balcony of the palace, overlooking the city's skyline. Seeing me go down on my knee made her cry, and through the tears, she said yes. Our moment was slightly perturbed by a city coming back to life and its usual vibes. "*Oi wanker, you can't park there*," said a van driver to another in passing, right below our balcony. We decided to elope and got married the next day. No more festivities with Sophie, now tired of the constant eye of the tabloids on us. There were only a few people invited. Gerrard, Patience, Chris, Charlotte and Mrs Patel. Mango was the ring bearer, and it proved to be a very tricky situation as all the jellied meat pouches in the world wouldn't persuade him to move towards us. Ultimately, it was Gerrard who picked him up and brought him over.

"I do," she said. And we never looked back.

Around the one-year mark, I got an interesting call from Border Control. I got into my vehicle and was driven to Heathrow, where a crowd of people, including journalists, were waiting outside the interrogation room. As I passed them, an officer asked me if I wanted to go in alone. I nodded, and he ushered me in.

Across the table, sat a long bearded Burlington, handcuffed but still wearing an immaculate suit, of course. His creepy smile returned once he saw me.

"Took you a while to get here," he said. "Traffic still bad in Dom's London?"

"One of the downsides of not trying to commit genocide is a packed city."

He shook his head and laughed.

"Genocide? You fool. We could've had a better society, a society that—"

I banged my fists on the table, interrupting his speech.

"Shut the fuck up!" I shouted. "You tried to kill us. Why did you come back?"

"Well, let bygones be bygones." He said. "Tusk kicked me out as he has a new political project in Germany, and I didn't know where to go. So, I made my way home." He lowered his gaze and played with the cuffs around his wrists. "I guess I just wanted to see if you would keep your word and kill me, as you threatened to a year ago?"

He looked at me as if trying to call my bluff. He only saw me as an idealist who could be manipulated and moulded. He was taunting me, and part of me wanted to give in, reach for my pistol and place a hole between his eye sockets.

"Come on, Dominic," he pressed, raising his voice. "Give these people what they came here for! Revenge! Show them you are capable."

I imagined myself grabbing my pistol and pressing it against his forehead. I could see it—his blood splattering across my shirt, the cold body slumping forward, the sound of the shot ringing in my ears. The journalists storming in, their cameras clicking like hungry vultures. Sophie looking at me, horrified.

"Not today, you bastard. I'll let your peers judge you and have them determine your sentence." I knock on the door for the officer to let me out. "I'm done with you."

As the door opened, I heard his voice crackle behind me, a mixture of desperation and bitterness. "You think this changes anything?" Burlington sneered, his voice hoarse. "I'll still be remembered long after you're gone. I am London! You...you're just a phase. A footnote." I paused in the doorway but didn't look back. His words didn't have the weight they used to. "You're nothing, Burlington. You're already forgotten."

I instructed the officer to take him into custody until the judge would set a date. The sensationalist journalists came forward as I stepped out of the room. "Matilda Vaughn from The Moon newspaper. Did you kill the leader of the Black Pyramids?"

With a straight face, I looked at her and said, "No, he is already dead to everyone in this city."

.....

It's been a long day packed with meetings in different parts of the city. Night has fallen by the time I return to my home office at the palace and pour myself a glass of whiskey. Sophie comes in, and I tell her about my day. "Sounds rough, do you want me to prepare you a bath?" I nod, and she blows me a kiss and makes her way to the bathroom. From Mango's room, squeaks and hisses can be heard. I step onto the balcony and see the lights from the O2 filling up the sky. I think it's a Taylor Swift concert. I scan the city as ambulances, shouts, and cheers can be heard vaguely from all over. I try to find the commune, but it seems to fade away in the distance and blend in with the rest of the city. Two years ago, all I wanted was to cook for a community where we make our own produce, unbothered and not bothering others. I have come full circle for one who has tried so much to escape this society and its hierarchical structures. More so, I have come full pyramid. For years, I fought against this. The idea of power, of control. I didn't want it then, and part of me still resents it now. The pyramid. It was always a symbol of everything wrong, everything corrupt. And yet, here I am, at the peak of it.

But maybe it's different now. Maybe it's what I do with it that matters. Power doesn't have to crush people. It doesn't have to be a weapon. Maybe, just maybe, I can reshape this pyramid. Turn it upside down. Support those who need it, raise up the people at the bottom.

"Bath is ready," says Sophie. "Mind if I join?"

I turn around and down the whisky, taking off my cufflinks. As I follow her, I admire her with each step she takes. Suddenly, my world feels smaller. She turns around and smiles at me, taking her robe off.

I follow her inside the steam-filled bathroom but turn briefly to take in one last look at the skyline behind me—London, my city, our city. The weight of the world can wait for now. Tonight, it's just us. And that's all I need.

The End.

WHAT TO EAT AFTER THY APOCALYPSE

DOMINIC HARGRAVES

The revolution is done. So... what's for dinner?

London,

I'm genuinely honoured (and still slightly confused) that the scrappy little collection of recipes I wrote during lockdown-fascism-survival mode actually found its way into your kitchens. Somehow, it made me... recognisable. People stop me at markets. Someone once asked me to sign a tin of lentils. Hounslow's overrun with food tourists. Please—there's only so much soup.

This new collection was put together for Cookfest, one year after the worst of it all. A celebration of survival, stubbornness, and sharing meals with people you might not agree with—but who still pass the salt.

The recipes here are simple and built around the most available ingredients across London. Whether your commune's got a proper oven or just a fire pit and good intentions, there's something here for you.

And I'm not the only one behind it. Chris, Gerrard, Sophie, Patience, Charlotte, and Mrs Patel have each contributed a dish—one memory, one method, one offering to the table. Because this was never just my kitchen.

I've always said food unites. That's why I'm sharing this now. Things feel tense again. The fractures are back. And no one's entirely sure who to trust anymore.

But food? Food still works.

Stick around after dessert.

It's the best part.

—Dom

Sophie's Leek & Potato Soup

Ingredients:

- 2 tbsp olive oil or butter
- 1 onion, chopped
- 2–3 leeks, sliced
- 3 medium potatoes, peeled and diced
- 1.2 L vegetable stock
- Salt & pepper

Instructions:

1. Sauté the onion and leeks until soft.
2. Add potatoes and stock, and simmer for 25 mins.
3. Blend or mash for the texture of choice.
4. Season and serve with bread.

Dom says:

"Sophie made this after a rough day for the commune. A cold snap caught us off guard, and we were all cuddled up in the Mess Hall. It helped us get through."

Charlotte's Classic Cottage Pie

Ingredients:

- 500g minced beef or plant-based mince
- 1 onion, chopped
- 2 carrots, diced
- 1 tbsp tomato purée
- 500ml beef stock
- 1 tbsp Worcestershire sauce (or soy sauce)
- 800g potatoes, peeled
- Butter & milk (or oil)
- Salt, pepper

Instructions:

1. Cook onion, carrot, and mince until browned.
2. Stir in tomato purée, stock, and sauce. Simmer 20 mins.
3. Boil potatoes, mash with butter and milk.
4. Layer the meat, then the mash, in a dish. Bake at 200°C for 20 mins.

Dom says:

"Watch out for Charlotte— she is a rising star. This recipe will make you feel like you are part of our commune."

Mrs Patel's Chana Masala

Ingredients:

- 1 can chickpeas
- 1 onion, finely chopped
- 2 garlic cloves, minced
- 1 tsp ginger
- 2 tomatoes, chopped, or 1/2 can
- 1 tsp cumin seeds
- 1/2 tsp turmeric
- 1 tsp garam masala
- 1/2 tsp ground coriander
- Salt, chilli to taste

Instructions:

1. Sauté cumin seeds, then onion, garlic, ginger until golden.
2. Add tomatoes and spices, cook into a paste.
3. Stir in chickpeas + 100ml water, simmer 15–20 mins.
4. Garnish with fresh coriander.

Dom says:

"Mrs Patel gave me this recipe, then told me to stay out of her kitchen. I still make it badly. She still eats it anyway."

Patience's Jamaican Rice and Peas

Ingredients:

- 1 cup long-grain rice
- 1 can of kidney beans
- 1 cup coconut milk
- 1 cup water
- 2 spring onions, thinly sliced
- 1 garlic clove minced
- 1 sprig thyme
- 1/2 scotch bonnet (optional) diced
- Salt to taste

Instructions:

1. Combine coconut milk, water, beans, garlic, onion, thyme, and pepper.
2. Simmer, then add rinsed rice and salt.
3. Stir once, cover, and simmer 20 mins until fluffy.
4. Remove thyme and pepper. Serve warm.

Dom says:

"Patience says this recipe is safe to include for all the white boys out there."

Dom's One-Pot Sausage & Bean Stew

Ingredients:

- 6 good-quality sausages (meat or plant-based)
- 1 onion, chopped
- 2 garlic cloves, minced
- 1 can chopped tomatoes
- 1 can white beans (cannellini or butter beans), drained
- 1 tsp smoked paprika
- 1 tsp dried thyme
- 1 tbsp tomato purée (optional)
- 250ml stock (veg or chicken)
- Salt, pepper, oil for frying

Instructions:

1. Brown sausages in a large pot with a bit of oil. Remove and slice into chunks (or leave whole if preferred). In the same pot, cook onion and garlic until soft.
2. Add tomato purée, paprika, and thyme. Stir and cook for 1 minute. Return sausages to the pot. Add chopped tomatoes, beans, and stock.
3. Simmer uncovered for 20–25 minutes until thick and bubbling.
4. Season to taste. Serve with bread, rice, or just spoons.

Dom says:

"This is what you make when people show up hungry, late, and with opinions. It shuts everyone up in the best way possible. Add chilli if you need to make a point."

Gerrard's Shakshuka

Ingredients:

- 1 tbsp olive oil
- 1 onion, chopped
- 1 red pepper, sliced
- 2 garlic cloves minced
- 1 tsp paprika
- 1/2 tsp cumin
- 1 can chopped tomatoes
- 4–6 eggs
- Salt, pepper
- Parsley (optional)

Instructions:

1. Sauté the onion and pepper until soft.
2. Add garlic, spices, and tomatoes; simmer 10 mins.
3. Make wells, crack eggs in. Cover and cook 6–8 mins.
4. Serve with bread. Eat while arguing about politics.

Dom says:

"Gerrard insists each egg represents a core principle of communal ethics. I just like it with toast."

Chris's Lemon Drizzle Cake (Ideal Vape Pairing: 'Citrus Ice')

Ingredients:

- 225g self-raising flour
- 225g butter or margarine
- 225g caster sugar
- 4 eggs
- Zest of 1 lemon
- Juice of 1 lemon
- 85g icing sugar

Instructions:

1. Cream butter and sugar. Beat in eggs, one at a time.
2. Fold in flour and lemon zest. Pour into loaf tin.
3. Bake at 180°C for 45–50 mins.
4. Mix lemon juice with icing sugar, pour over warm cake.

Dom says:

"Chris swears this cake enhances vape flavours. I say it's just bloody good cake."

BONUS RECIPE

LONDON CRUMBLE

(Serves: 9 million, if we get it right)

Ingredients:

- One city, still aching after the fallout of the revolution;
- A populist with too much charisma and no morals;
- A handful of angry men in black;
- One tech feudalist, controlling all our information;
- One mass of frightened citizens looking for simple answers;
- Memories (optional, but recommended)
- A generous pinch of courage
- Zero tolerance for fascists

Instructions:

1. Preheat your paranoia. Stir the pot just enough so neighbours stop trusting one another.
2. Fold in catchy slogans like *"Make Britain British Again"* and *"Strength Through Order."* Watch it rise quickly and collapse just as fast.
3. Toss in some "others" to blame: immigrants, artists, teachers, the bloke down the street with the funny accent.
4. Bake under pressure, in echo chambers.

5. Serve with fear. Keep the masses hungry for certainty.

But here's the twist:

We've seen this dish before. We know what it tastes like. And it's bitter.

London,

I won't sugarcoat it. We are once again in danger. This time, not from bombs or barricades, but ballots. The Black Pyramids offer us a burnt crust of "order," but inside, it's all rot.

You may know me as a cook, not a candidate. And believe me, I'd rather be in Hounslow making stew. But apathy is a spice fascists thrive on. If we do nothing, they will serve us another regime wrapped in a Union Jack and call it a meal.

Don't believe me? Check what Gerrard found at **www.blackpyramidexposed.wordpress.com**

What I Want

I want freedom.

The freedom to walk home without fear. To speak your mind without being branded an enemy. To live your truth without needing someone else's permission.

I want a city where difference isn't just tolerated, it's

welcomed.

Where your name, your accent, and your story don't make you a target. They make you part of the whole.

I want unity. Not uniformity.

We don't all have to think the same, pray the same, or eat the same.

But we do need to remember we're in this together, through thick and thin.

I want us to stay awake because we've been here before.

It started with a few speeches, some promises about strength, tradition, and control.

It sounded reasonable, familiar.

"Make Britain Great Again."

What followed was silence, fear, and loss.

Of rights. Of neighbours. Of ourselves.

The Black Pyramids want to finish what that movement started.

They talk about order, but they mean obedience.

They offer structure, but it's a cage.

And once it's built, you don't get to pick which side

of the bars you're on.

I'm not running to lead. I'm running to stop them.

I want to live in a place where we share what we have: stories, meals, streets without suspicion.

Where your neighbour is someone you talk to, not just nod at behind a locked door.

This isn't about left or right anymore.

Will we build something honest, or will we let them bulldoze what's left?

You know who I am. I've got no interest in power.

So I'm standing. For my city. For the people who fed me when I had nothing.

For those who know that doing nothing is how *they* win.

Vote against fear. Vote against forgetting. Vote for freedom.

Let's get our city back.

Dom

ACKNOWLEDGMENTS

It takes a village to write a book.

I couldn't have brought this sequel to life without the support of many people along the way.

First, the moral (and often technical) support.

Bushra, my love, thank you for your endless encouragement and for putting up with me through every stage of this journey. When I'm down, you pick me up. When I'm up, you keep me there. I'm endlessly grateful.

To my **family, my parents and sister**, for always believing in me. For supporting me through my highs and lows.

To my **friends**, thank you for being there when I needed you, for cheering me on, and for reminding me to sleep. In particular, **Dragos and Siana**, thank you for always showing up. Brief thanks to **Mango**, too, for letting me use his image rights.

To the readers (turned friends) who became part of this

book's creation.

Laura and Joy, thank you for your countless notes, nudges, and edits.

My **beta readers**: **Ash, Ed, Andrew, and Mellissa**. Your guidance as readers and Mango enjoyers helped me shape the sequel.

And finally, perhaps most importantly, **to you**, the reader. There would be no sequel without the thousands of you who read *What to Eat During the Apocalypse* and helped it find its place in the world.

I didn't know what to expect when I released that first book. But what I received was the best welcome. You've supported me, shared your thoughts, posted reviews, and sent kind, funny, and moving messages. You've reminded me why I write.

I'm so grateful that this story has made you laugh, made you reflect, or helped you see your communities—and your role in shaping them—a little differently.

While the *What to Eat* universe may be coming to a close, I have more stories to tell.

I'd love for you to be part of the journey.

Let's keep in touch:

@vladimirstefan_ on socials

www.vladimir-stefan.co.uk

www.ingramcontent.com/pod-product-compliance
Lightning Source LLC
Chambersburg PA
CBHW020340010526
44119CB00048B/535